Advance Praise for
Relax With Life

"Kenyon's very readable, engaging style shows you how to simply and powerfully make the steps to change your experience of life. Before you know it, you will have received core tools to use the ancient teachings of yoga in the midst of everyday challenges."

~ Kamini Desai PhD, author of
Life Lessons Love Lessons

"In this book the author brilliantly interweaves her use of yoga techniques for stress reduction in her own personal life, including during times of major life transitions. Subsequently, the reader quickly understands how these strategies can effectively address any number of things that cause stress in one's life. This is a must-have resource for dealing with many of the most common sources of stress today."

~ Susan Dennison, Associate Professor, University of North Carolina at Greensboro

"With courageous candor and gentle humor, Kenyon offers both a lucid and logical look at the real sources of stress in our everyday lives, gifting us with simple, concrete techniques for lasting transformation. If we utilize these powerful *yogic* tools, we can come to accept any life situation and discover the underlying "peace beneath the turmoil." Stress-eliminating applications intertwine with heart-opening personal illustrations, making *Relax with Life* a veritable handbook not only for life, but also for living joyously. Empowering, inspiring, and illuminating!"

~ Laura Harsha Conley, Director of the Learning Center, Canterbury School of Florida, Board Member, Seva Yoga Outreach

"Kenyon spent several years with a Living Yoga Master, learning firsthand how to embody the ancient teachings of yoga. This deceptively simple discourse allows readers, both in the East and West, to see how yoga can be applied practically in our day-to-day lives."

~ Yasin M. Choudry, M.D., Diplomat American Board of Psychiatry and Neurology

"Kenyon makes the profound teachings of yoga both relevant and accessible to everyone, regardless of whether they practice yoga or not. I have been able to apply these ideas more effectively in my own life through her clear explanations and, most of all, through the examples from her life. I plan to share readings from this book with my own students."

~ Laura Angira Gushin,
Yoga Instructor, E-RYT 500

"Yoga has long been used as an effective tool to reduce stress; this book will show you a personal path for doing so. Kenyon is walking the walk; not afraid to share her vulnerable moments for the sake of helping others see the deep wisdom in her *yogic* path. If you are curious, in transition, or just plain fed up with things as they are—read this book. It is a thoughtful, deep-dive into the power that yoga offers for transformation. The writing is clear, accessible, and inspirational."

~ Susan Freeman, Author of *Step Up Now*

"Every once in a while, a book comes out that combines practical 'how-to' descriptions with narrative story and spiritual principles. This is one of those rare books. Kenyon merges body, mind, and spirit in a very useable way. She is a clear writer and sincerely wants all of us to "right" our lives. The sharing of her personal story along with insightful ways to relax with life and apply *yogic* principles to reduce stress is a book everyone will benefit from and actually use. This book offers inspiration, transformation, and most of all, practical tools to use in our often chaotic lives. Thank you, Kenyon, for writing it."

~ Moe Ross, CEO and Founder of Miographies,
Author, Spiritual Director at
Hollyhock Retreat Center

"Kenyon's book reveals practical spiritual tools to help you respond to life with skill and grace. Throughout her book she weaves *yogic* philosophy with her personal life experiences, which allows all to resonate and relate."

~ John Vosler, body worker, business owner

"What a wonderful explanation of the mind, body, spirit totality that is a true yoga practice. Bringing this to us, Kenyon Gatlin gives us all strategies for dealing with suffering and for finding peace. I wish this book had been available to me when I was dealing with the crises of working in a domestic violence shelter."

~ Margaret Anglin, Executive Director (Retired), Harbor House, Orange County Center Against Domestic Violence

Relax With Life

Applying Yoga Principles to Reduce Stress

By Kenyon Gatlin

Love Your Life

Love Your Life

Love Your Life Publishing

Wilmington, DE

www.loveyourlifepublishing.com

ISBN: 978-1-934509-84-5

Library of Congress Control Number: 2015931352

Printed in the United States of America

First Printing 2015

Cover design by 2FacedDesign.com

Editing by Suzanne Gochenouer

Photography by Russell T. Mobley

This book is dedicated to you and me

Table of Contents

Preface

This book is a culmination of my understanding and practice of spiritual yoga taught to me by *Yogi* Amrit Desai, who has been my teacher since 2005. *Yogi* Desai came to America from India in 1960, dedicating over fifty-four years to teaching how to apply the ancient science of yoga to modern-day society. In January of 2012, I moved into his *ashram*, and lived and studied there for several years, working in various departments. Over the last few years of that time, I worked as his personal secretary and office manager.

I have been teaching yoga since 2001. I am registered with the Yoga Alliance as an Experienced Registered Yoga Teacher at the 200 level (E-RYT 200) and the 500 level (RYT-500). In addition, I am a yoga *nidra* facilitator, and certified in yoga therapeutics.

Through *Yogi* Desai's teachings, I have learned the power of authentic yoga, which means relaxing with whatever is before me. In this process of relaxing with my emotions and circumstances, I have released my deep fears and anxieties, even cured my arachnophobia. I began to experience "the peace that surpasses understanding" mentioned in the Bible.

As I did so, I noticed it came with a joy and freshness that Buddhists refer to as "beginner's mind."

Long before meeting *Yogi* Desai, I was a spiritual seeker, reading books by Deepak Chopra, Thich Nhat Hanh, Pema Chodron, Jack Kornfield, along with many others. Although I loved those books, and found them inspiring, I wondered how the authors applied the practice in *their* lives. This was the main inspiration for writing this book.

I am an ordinary woman who uses simple yoga techniques to practice relaxing with life. In this book, I share with you my journey of taking yoga off the mat. Through my experiences, you will learn the true meaning of relaxing, how it can lead you to freedom from your fears, frustrations, and anxieties, toward a "peace that surpasses understanding" and a love of life.

Introduction

The sixth-grade dance was the most awkward moment of my twelve-year old life. As I watched my peers have fun, I noticed my clothes looked nothing like theirs. I wasn't familiar with the popular songs, and felt too self-conscious to dance. That night I deeply felt I didn't belong.

I took mental notes so I could learn to fit in with my peers. When I got home, I listened to the radio, recorded the popular songs, wrote down the lyrics and memorized them. I went to the mall and bought trendier clothes. Yet no matter what I did externally, on the inside, I was an awkward outsider.

Throughout much of my life, I felt like an actor in a play, missing some key information about my role. What was the point of life? What was this play all about, anyway?

Several years after college, I strongly desired answers to that missing information about this play called Life. Outwardly, I had everything going for me. I had a good career, was in a loving relationship, and enjoyed where I was living. Despite this, I felt a general discontent, a lack of purpose. Without understanding why, I felt life had to be bigger than the role I played, yet I didn't know any other way to live.

One day, on my hour-long commute home from work, I said a prayer to a God I sort of believed in. It didn't matter that I only somewhat believed, what mattered was that it was heartfelt. I wanted to know "Is this all there is? Is this all life is about?" On the outside, everything was great. Inside, I felt disconnected from life, purposeless. I really meant it when I cried out that evening, "Is this it?" That cry to the Universe was the beginning of my inner journey into meaning and spiritual practice, the beginning of relaxing with life while discovering the joy and freedom life offers.

Within a week, I came across several books by Neale Donald Walsch. I was browsing in the spirituality category of my favorite bookstore when, suddenly, all the books on the shelf seemed to disappear except for a series of three books called *Conversations with God*. During this bizarre experience, I felt drawn to flip through one. I immediately knew I was meant to read those books. After reading Walsch's books, I was motivated to find a meditation class. The yoga and meditation class I found wasn't really what I wanted, but it was the only thing available. Of course, it turned out to be exactly what I needed. I didn't realize until taking that class that yoga is much more than poses. Thus began my life-long process of diving deeper into the spiritual aspect of yoga, learning to use the practice off the mat, in my daily life.

This book takes you through my personal journey of using the integrative techniques of yoga in the midst of my life: at work, in relationships, traffic jams, lay-offs, illness, with my fear, my anger, my joy, and my happiness. This practice has carried me through hardships and crises, has connected me to life, and to living. I have used these techniques of yoga to help me be at peace with whatever arises in each moment. As I practice relaxing with each experience, I've discovered a loving power deep within me that can handle anything.

Most of us cannot get away to a monastery, *ashram*, or mountain cave. We must learn to practice with the distraction, excitement, chaos, and even crises of everyday life. As you read how I have integrated yoga into my life, you will have a clearer understanding of how to practice in the midst of your own daily distractions, and how to use this practice to relax with your life.

Whatever tradition or religion you practice or belong to, or even if you do not have a tradition or religion, these yoga techniques can assist you in living life to its fullest. The integrative practice of yoga allows you to experience the entirety of the moment, reducing suffering, increasing contentment and joy.

THREE CORE YOGA TECHNIQUES

Typically, yoga is defined as union. Yet you cannot practice union, as it is the end result of yoga. The practice of yoga is actually integration, *moving toward* union, or wholeness. As you practice integration with your experiences, one moment at a time, you are practicing relaxation. Yoga is a system of relaxation, which moves you toward wholeness and a fulfilling, complete experience of your life. This is how yoga heals the mind, body, and psyche.

As you become more relaxed, integrating with your life, your body, heart, mind, and soul become fully engaged in all you do or experience. You are complete in your experience of life, totally present with what is before you. Normally, you think one thing, feel another, and do a third. No wonder we are stressed out! When every part of you is present in the moment, you are relaxed, even in the midst of activity.

The three core yoga techniques that help dissolve stress, returning you to relaxation and integration are:

1. Witnessing your thoughts and emotions.
2. Feeling the physical sensations in your body.
3. Deepening and connecting to your breath.

These are simple yet powerful techniques. Their simplicity makes them easy to remember. Although I will explain them separately, they are to be practiced simultaneously. I will give examples of how to do that throughout this book. As you read my explanations of the techniques, along with how I have applied them in my life, it will become clear how to practice yoga.

BEGINNING A PRACTICE

These techniques can be practiced anywhere, while doing anything. Nevertheless, I encourage you to begin in pleasant or neutral circumstances. Do not expect to be successful with crisis situations in the beginning, as that is not realistic. For example, you do not begin weight lifting with 200 pounds. If you are new to weight lifting, you start by bench pressing just the bar. Once you build strength with that, you add several pounds of weight. As you keep gaining in strength, you are able to add more weight.

Beginning your practice with crises would be comparable to lifting a lot of weight, therefore impossible to accomplish. These techniques will be available to you in a crisis after you have some experience practicing them in easier situations. Instead of physical weight lifting, you are doing psychological weight lifting. As you observe yourself, and practice these techniques, you will be able to relax, becoming more at peace in all situations, including any crisis.

Your life is your practice. These techniques of witnessing, feeling sensations in your body, and breathing, do not require you to make extra time in your schedule. However, they do require you to pay attention throughout the day. Any experience during your daily routine will give you ample opportunity to practice.

Practice as you walk from your front door to your car, as you brush your teeth, load the dishwasher, or when stuck in traffic. The easiest times to practice these techniques are in neutral situations such as your daily routines. There is nothing bothering you in these situations except your thoughts.

The next level of difficulty is with slightly irritating situations, then with upsetting situations, and lastly crisis situations. As you practice these techniques, relax. Experience the peace beneath the turmoil of difficult situations, as well as the peace and joy of pleasant situations. You are usually so caught up in your thoughts that you even miss the joy in pleasant experiences!

PURPOSE OF THE YOGA MAT

Although most of this book is about how to practice yoga in everyday life, I do include a section on formal practice. Working on a yoga mat provides a controlled environment in which to use these techniques. It is like conducting experiments in a laboratory before taking these techniques into the uncontrolled environment of life.

As with anything new you are learning, it is helpful to start simply and work your way up. When you learn to play music you first learn chords and simple melodies. Next, you have fun playing more complicated pieces. The same is true when learning these core yoga techniques. Practicing one or two poses using the core techniques will help you take these techniques to the more challenging environment of daily life.

Then instead of practicing with Chair pose on your mat, you are practicing with "traffic jam" pose on the road, or "children fighting" pose at home.

THE EDGE

I use the term "edge" throughout this book. It is where your ability to relax intersects with your tendency to become tense and react. A reaction happens when you are uncomfortable and act out mentally, verbally or physically. To practice at the edge, feel the sensations of discomfort, and apply the yoga techniques to relax with it, instead of acting out (reacting).

You grow the most when you are on your edge, when you feel discomfort but choose to relax with it. The edge allows you to practice being at peace with what is before you. As you relax on your edge, you find situations that used to bother you no longer do. Your edges keep growing outward as you feel relaxed with more people and situations. You experience more freedom as your boundaries expand, giving you more space to live peacefully.

Chapter

I

Witnessing Thoughts and Feelings

THE POWER OF THOUGHTS

Thoughts are powerful; therefore, it is important to be aware of what you are thinking. You assume your thoughts are benign, yet they actually create your reality. For example, have you ever mistaken a leaf, or a clump of thread, for a spider or bug? It likely caused you to jump, and your heart to race. It is as if the spider really existed, even though it was only your imagination.

You can be in the safety of your home, but worried about your finances, or remembering what someone did to you last month. Soon your heart is racing, your blood pressure rising. You feel anxious. On the other hand, you can reminisce about a wonderful trip you took a couple of years ago, and soon you are smiling and feeling good.

You experience life through the filter of your thoughts. You have probably been to a movie with a friend and really enjoyed it, whereas your friend did not. Perhaps you went to an event that you liked, but overheard someone else complain about it. Maybe you have been on a date and had a lousy time, but your date had fun and wanted to go out with you again. Perhaps you said something to a friend and were surprised by his reaction; he heard something different from what you said. Even eyewitnesses at a crime scene will give different accounts of what happened.

Since everyone has different thoughts, concepts, and beliefs, we have different experiences of the same event. No one experiences the event directly; you experience your thoughts about the event. The thought filter is similar to wearing yellow glasses. You experience the world as yellow, so you believe it is yellow.

Most of the time, your thoughts and the way you interpret reality create stress. **Without a conscious practice, you live what you think about life, instead of living life as it is.** The constant projections, expectations, anticipations, worries, and anxieties of your unconscious thoughts leave you drained and exhausted. The majority of your thoughts are so full of worry about the future, or regrets about the past, that you miss the only place life can be lived: the present.

While walking in the woods, you may worry about the meeting you are leading tomorrow, or about your dwindling savings.

Worry and anxiety do nothing to solve problems or change a situation. They only create resistance, causing you to feel stressed and stuck. Meanwhile, you are missing the smell of the pine trees, the touch of the earth beneath your feet, and the sound of the birds as you walk. No wonder you do not enjoy your life!

By the end of the walk, you are tired, instead of refreshed, because you were not present with your walk. The stress created by this constant worry can become a daily destructive habit. This is why it is so important to bring attention to your thoughts.

When you notice your thoughts, you realize you cannot be your thoughts. You notice the lamp on your dresser; therefore, you know you are separate from the lamp. When you notice your friend, you know you are separate; you are not your friend. If you imagine a ship, you know you are not the ship. You are the one who has the thought of a ship. The same is true for any of your thoughts and emotions. Once you realize this, you have the power to change your thoughts, thereby changing your life.

Albert Einstein said, "No problem can be solved from the same level of consciousness that created it." When you witness your thoughts, you tap into a higher consciousness that can solve your problems. You tap into the One who notices your thoughts. The practice of witnessing your thoughts and feelings helps you detach from your personal drama so you can experience life as it really is, rather than living your perceptions about life. Noticing thoughts gives you the space to make choices and respond, in place of reacting.

CREATING YOUR REALITY

You have probably experienced saying something to someone who completely misunderstood what you said. They didn't hear what you said; rather they heard what they *thought* you said. I was amused while observing this with my close friends one day.

Liz was driving us back from the beach while her husband Jake rested in the passenger seat. Liz decided to get off at a different exit than the one they usually take.

Jake perked up and asked, "Where are we?"

Liz explained that she took a different exit to save a little on the tolls.

"Oh." Jake went back to resting.

"What?"

"Nothing," said Jake. "I didn't say anything."

"Yes, you did." Liz insisted, "You think I should have taken the exit we usually use."

"No, I didn't say anything."

Liz's voice got louder as she exclaimed, "You always think your way is the better way to go…"

I finally interjected to tell Liz that Jake really didn't say anything.

"Oh shut up, Kenyon. Stay out of this," retorted Liz.

"Yeah," said Jake. "Kenyon, stay out of this. Liz is having an argument with herself."

This is what we all do. We bring our past experiences into the present moment. Once we do that, we don't experience and respond to the present, but to our past. We hear with our thoughts, not with our ears.

To experience life directly, you need to relax with how you feel. This is not easy because, naturally, you don't want to feel uncomfortable, scared, or sad. However, if you don't allow yourself to experience those emotions, you won't be able to experience joy, peace, and happiness either.

Watching your thoughts and emotions from the detached place of the witness, feeling the pure sensations in the body from the emotion or experience, and breathing deeply, will help you stay with what you "think" is uncomfortable. Your rigid opinions about what you like—or don't like—begin to soften, allowing you to relax more with everything. You do not have to waste all your energy trying to keep what you like and avoid what you don't like. You can simply live your life, instead of constantly trying to manage what you ultimately can't control anyway.

THE WITNESS IS THE SEER

The witness is the part of you that observes your thoughts, feelings, and actions. It is a higher consciousness, or field of awareness that is within you and outside of you. There is nowhere this field of awareness does not exist. You tap into this consciousness when you practice witnessing.

The witness does not judge or criticize; rather, it watches your judgments, criticisms, likes, and dislikes. It is a blank canvas. **You create your life and reality by consciously, or unconsciously, painting physical, mental, or emotional forms onto this blank canvas.** The witness is the omnipresent field that simply shows you what you have created. It does not have an opinion about your creations.

Remember, you are not your thoughts. If you were your thoughts, you would not be capable of watching them, just like your eyes cannot see themselves because they are what sees. Your eyes can only see their reflection in the mirror. You are the witness, the field of awareness, the higher consciousness behind the thoughts, capable of observing everything you think, feel, and do. **You are what you cannot see.**

Try this experiment as you read this book—begin to notice your thoughts about what you read. Simply watch and notice them. There is a part of you that can observe yourself reading this book and having thoughts about what you read. There is a part of you that can notice what you think and feel. That part of you is the witness.

This higher consciousness, or witness, does not require you to do anything. It simply shows you what is there, without judgment or comment. When you turn on a light so you can see, the light does not judge or comment; it simply shines. So it is with the witness. It is like sunshine illuminating a ditch in the road. When you see the ditch, you can walk around it. If you are not paying attention and fall into the ditch, the sunshine will not comment about it. It will simply continue to shine, illuminating where you lie.

Now that you see yourself lying in the ditch, you have a choice. You can climb out or you can continue lying there. The light doesn't care what you choose. It will show you that you have a choice. If you don't know you are lying in a ditch, you do not have the choice to climb out of it.

The witness shows you where you are. If you want to go to a new store in the mall, you look at the directory to find it. Once you locate the store on the directory map, you must also find the dot that marks "You are here." Only then can you move in the direction of the store. Once you know where you are in life, you can move in the direction you want to go.

When you don't know where you are, you move around aimlessly, never reaching your destination. Most of us do not know where we are, so we cannot move in the right direction to get where we want to go. When you know where you are, you have a choice in setting your direction.

This nonjudgmental watching is a powerful force that can change your life when you tap into it. It can help you fully live and enjoy life, rather than cowering in darkness and fear, or hiding behind your anger. When you are fearful, you can experience the fear through the witness, and allow it to move out. You realize you are not your fear. The witness removes the drama from your thoughts, emotions, and stories. Once it is gone, you gain clarity and insight about your situation. Suffering becomes much less painful when there is no drama.

Witnessing allows you to dispassionately observe your mental patterns and situations. It anchors you in the present moment where there is nothing to worry about, because there is only certainty in the present. All your worries, regrets, and hopes take you into the past or future, preventing you from living in the present.

FOUR LEVELS OF CONSCIOUSNESS

There are four levels of consciousness. Two are below the mind: unconscious and subconscious. You are not aware of what is happening on these levels. The third level is waking-consciousness, where we make decisions and interact with the world. The last level is super-consciousness, above the waking-conscious.

The unconscious stores your beliefs, concepts, feelings, and memories. You are not aware of anything in the unconscious, but it influences your waking-conscious behavior. Because these beliefs are below the conscious mind you cannot access them. You might be aware that you don't like a situation, yet because you've unconsciously created it, it is impossible to make a permanent and lasting change. You can't understand how you had anything to do with creating your situation, because it comes from below the level of the mind. Since you don't know how you created it, you can't create something different.

For example, you want to be successful, but you have an unconscious belief that you are not good enough. No matter how talented you are, or what you do to get ahead, this hidden belief keeps you from being successful.

The subconscious is also below the level of the mind. Unlike unconsciousness, it is in harmony with nature and the universe. Our survival level instincts reside in the subconscious, but they are balanced and natural. When these instincts are superimposed onto our unconscious beliefs about ourselves, or others, they become distorted and out of balance. The natural instinct for sex can become an addiction, or aversion, to sex. The natural instinct to eat can become an obsession, creating anorexia or obesity.

Your consciousness is your ego mind that has thoughts, analysis, judgments, opinions, and emotions. Most of us live and create from ego-mind consciousness. Ego is never satisfied for long, so frequently our creations do not achieve lasting happiness or peace. When we are happy with what we have, there is often a subtle, or not so subtle, underlying fear of losing it.

Because of that fear of loss, we attempt to control and manage life in such a way that we can keep what we like. This takes a lot of effort and manipulation, which ultimately keeps us from true happiness.

The witness is super-consciousness, and is above the level of the mind. It is the blank field that shows you your consciousness. When you tap into the witness, your creations no longer come from the fear-based creations of ego, but from the field of creative, pure potential.

Because the witness is the light of awareness, it can illuminate what is in the darkness of unconscious. As it brings the unconscious into your consciousness, you can now work to clear the misconceptions and beliefs that influence your behavior. That is why the witness is so important. It is the only level of consciousness that can access and clear what is unconscious.

PRACTICING THE WITNESS

To practice connecting to the witness, bring your attention to your thoughts and emotions (or feelings). Simply observe them as though they are passing clouds. Notice if your thoughts or emotions are positive, negative, worrisome, judgmental, or reoccurring. You might notice there are so many thoughts you can hardly separate one from the other. They are just constant mental noise.

Noticing the thoughts or mental noise without doing anything about it will automatically create a shift in your mind. It is similar to when you know the police are usually patrolling a certain area. You automatically slow down. The witness acts as a policeman. It does not give tickets; it just watches. When the mind knows it is being watched, it starts to slow down a bit.

As you watch the mind, if you don't like what you see, notice that as well, and continue watching. Remember, the witness just shows you what is there; it is your ego-mind that judges. Even if you don't like what you see, it is only when you see it that you have the choice to change it.

As you witness, it is like shining a bright light into a dark, neglected room. When the room is illuminated and you can see, you know what you need to do to clean the room and reclaim it. As you shine the light of your awareness into the darkness, the darkness automatically disappears. Darkness cannot exist in light so don't worry, just keep watching, and the light of your attention will dissolve what is there.

Anger, sadness, worry, and emotions like these, are all types of darkness that cannot exist in light. Therefore, over time, those types of thoughts simply dissolve in the light of your consciousness. You do not have to resist the dark; it is not bad. Just watch it. Without darkness, you wouldn't be able to know or experience light. There would be no frame of reference for the light without the dark.

Watch your thoughts, feelings, and actions during simple, neutral activities or situations. Witness your thoughts as you walk to your car, as you fold the laundry, or you brush your teeth. As you practice during these basic situations, you will be able to watch yourself experience nervousness on a job interview, or while giving a presentation. You can watch your reaction when you are frustrated in traffic, or when someone insults you. Observe as a witness, so you don't get caught up in your nervousness, fear, or anger. You not only watch your thoughts, but also your feelings, and the pure sensations in the body. Breathe, to relax with what you feel and think.

In the beginning, during challenging situations, you will likely react first, before you notice. As soon as you notice you are in reaction, watch and feel the effects this has in your body and mind. With practice, you will be able to watch yourself while you react, and eventually, before you react. At some point, you won't even have a reaction. The person or situation will no longer affect you.

If you have been negative for a long time, it will be hard, at first, to reverse this. A part of you wants to stay negative. Notice this by witnessing your negativity. Remember that the witness does not do anything except watch and show you where you are. That alone will slow the momentum, making it easier to replace your thoughts at some point, if you choose to do so.

When you resist something, you feed energy into it and it will persist. Do not resist what you see, just observe it; allow the resistance to exist as it is. Witness the pure sensations of resistance as felt in your body. Notice the tightening in the throat, constriction in the chest, the heat, or the knot in the stomach. Allow yourself to experience these sensations from the perspective of the witness. Breathe, to relax with the experience. It is not nearly as bad as the story your mind spins about the sensations.

As you practice, you will notice that you enjoy complaining or acting out at times. You might observe yourself gossiping, but not want to stop. You will notice you do not want to practice. There are times I can see myself having a reaction to a situation. I know I could stop myself, but I don't. There is a part of me enjoying my reaction. I watch myself enjoy my reaction, and watch myself regret it later. This is okay; no one is perfect.

Simply watch and feel your resistance. It will eventually dissolve. Do not fight with yourself and your resistance to doing your practice, as you will only strengthen the resistance. Just watch, and see what begins to happen. As you witness and bring your awareness to the feeling of resistance, it is like a beam of sunlight reflected through a magnifying glass. When you align the resistance, or any other emotion, under the magnifying glass of the witness, it will catch fire and burn away.

You might think witnessing, watching yourself, and observing your thoughts, will cause life to be boring. I have found the opposite to be true. Since we are caught in our thoughts all the time, we do not even experience life. We experience our thoughts about life. As you connect to the witness, you disengage from your mental filter, and begin to experience life as it is. Life becomes fresh and fascinating.

Instead of needing the stimulus of excitement to feel alive, you feel alive in every moment. You begin to feel joyful and peaceful while walking to your car, cooking dinner, having lunch with friends, or relaxing on your patio.

There are so many blessings for which to be joyful. You do not need to wait for the exciting once-in-a-while big event, you can rejoice now. I have found that many of the things I used to do for fun are now over-stimulating and draining. They provided an exciting escape, which in the end left me tired. I much prefer the peace and joy found in simple things. When you live life directly, you do not need to escape it.

CHANGE YOUR THOUGHTS / CHANGE YOUR EXPERIENCE

You cannot change what you do not see. Simply because you do not see something doesn't mean it isn't affecting your life. As you notice your thoughts and emotions, and remove the drama and the stories, you can change your behavior or stay the same. You have a choice. Sometimes you might choose to remain in negativity, but there is a difference when the choice is yours.

Since what you experience is predominantly through the filter of your thoughts, replacing negative thoughts with positive thoughts can be a powerful practice. When people are frequently angry or sad, it shows in their body and posture. They have a hostile or depressed energy. There are expressive lines etched in their face. Their posture is rigid and defensive. Other people consciously, or subconsciously, recognize this demeanor, and respond to it. When you are angry, the people you attract tend to be angry and defensive too, and you will often find yourself in hostile or difficult situations that escalate your anger.

Positive, happy people have a gentle demeanor with a pleasant look on their face, which attracts others similar in nature. Therefore, they find themselves in more pleasant situations, where people are kind to each other. Your energy, thoughts, and actions show themselves in your physical appearance. Life reflects that back to you. If you do not know how you are behaving, or what you are expressing, look at the people and situations around you.

This is a key reason why practicing the witness is such a powerful tool for changing your life. When you observe your thoughts, you have the power to change them. Change your thoughts and you change your energy. When you can do that, your actions, and their results, quickly follow suit. You will attract different people and experiences to yourself. When you watch from the perspective of the witness, changes occur naturally and effortlessly. It is not a forced change, it just happens as a result of your observation. The following are two examples of how I used the witness to change my experience.

THE WINTER OF 2010

I grew up in Miami, Florida, and am not fond of cold weather. In January of 2010, I was laid off from work and living in a poorly insulated house in North Carolina. I collected unemployment, so money was tight. I could not afford to heat the house. Often, I would wear thermal underwear, a wool sweater, coat, scarf, hat, and gloves, but still felt quite cold. There were days I could see my breath in the house! It was a challenge to chop vegetables and prepare meals with my cold hands. My thoughts quickly nose-dived into "Poor me… life sucks… I have no money… I'm so miserable…" After I observed this for a while, I decided to climb out of the ditch of negative thinking.

I changed my attitude by using a gratitude practice. I shifted my thoughts to "How lucky I am that I have this coat and hat. I am healthy. I have a working car, a couch to sit on, an electric blanket to sleep under, and a comfortable bed."

When I took a bath or shower, I reminded myself how fortunate I was to have such an abundance of warm water. When it rained, I was thankful for the dry roof over my head.

It wasn't long before I experienced a shift and began feeling really good. I even felt rather wealthy. By noticing my negative thoughts, and changing them to positive ones, I changed my whole outlook and experience of the situation.

What makes the gratitude practice effective is that you place your attention on what is positive, instead of trying to convince yourself you are happy when you are cold and miserable. By focusing on the positive, I *felt* positive. I could be happy even while cold.

If you are upset about having to wash the dishes, or clean the kitchen, think about how grateful you are to have two strong legs to stand on, indoor plumbing, electricity to provide warm soapy water, clean dishtowels, a sink, and a dry roof over your head. When you think about it, no matter what your situation, there is something in your life for which you can be grateful. It is impossible to be negative with so much gratitude.

LAYING A BRICK PATH

Another powerful experience I've had with gratitude was during a landscape project. My husband had severe health problems and could not help much with physical labor. One hot day I was outside, making a brick path. I used a pickaxe to break up the hard North Carolina clay, and dug a level depression so I could later add the sand and lay the bricks. I was tired, sore, and feeling sorry for myself because I had no help. I fought with reality, wishing I were not doing this hard labor, but made myself do it anyway. My negative thoughts about the situation soon dragged me down.

About that time, my husband came out of the house to see how my efforts were going. He pointed out some areas that were not level and places that needed to be dug deeper. Well, that put me over my edge. I went into reaction. I let him have it and told him where he could go! I could see the hurt on his face from my reaction, and immediately felt horrible about my outburst. He couldn't help it that he had no strength due to his poor health. I knew he felt bad that he wasn't able to help. My reaction just made him feel worse. I went in the house to apologize. I really was very sorry for the way I had treated him.

Back from my apology, I resumed my work with the pickaxe. This time I remembered my gratitude practice. I thought about how grateful I was to have health, strength, and flexibility. My good health allowed me to do hard work that many people, including my husband, weren't able to do.

As I focused my attention on these new thoughts, all of a sudden I was flooded with energy, peace, and bliss. I was so happy to be out there working hard! With all the energy

I suddenly had, I got a lot done in a short time. I couldn't believe how good I felt, how easy the work was. The soreness I felt before was also gone, and I felt fine in the following days, too.

Being grateful connected me to the loving, healing source of life, to the energy that sustains existence. That source will allow you to do amazing things. It gave me the power to finish the brick path quickly, healed my sore muscles and achy body, in addition to filling me with peace and bliss.

CONNECT TO THE WITNESS, CONNECT TO GOD

Most people believe or disbelieve in God, then assume God does or doesn't exist. Yet this is just a concept of God that you accept or reject, neither is the experience of God. Change your idea of God if the concept you have doesn't work for you. If it works for you, then keep it, but be open to change as you gain experience and knowledge of God.

God is omniscient, omnipotent, and omnipresent. The energy that makes up life and sustains existence fits that description. You can physically connect to energy when you connect to your breath, which is the main carrier of energy. We tend to think breath is just oxygen. If that were the case, you could pump oxygen into a cadaver and it would come back to life.

Breathe deeply. Feel the pulsations and tingles of energy course through your body. Experience the energy by bringing your attention to it.

If you don't connect with the concept of energy, think of God as a higher consciousness. That also fits with omniscient, omnipotent, and omnipresent. Pay attention. Notice the intelligence of life. There is a consciousness, or force, that knows how to continue breathing when you are unconscious in sleep. It causes your body to shift positions while you sleep, your heart to pump, and your blood to circulate. It causes a plant to grow and a flower to bloom. It supports the bird that glides on air currents, and the dragonfly that hovers and darts among the weeds. Don't try to analyze it, just marvel at the wonder of it. Observe nature. Observe yourself.

Breathe fully and be present. Get out of your head. Most people think and analyze too much. Not that thinking is bad, but God cannot be understood with the head. You will not find God by thinking. God is found by feeling, experiencing, and paying attention. Notice how things big and small manifest for you.

I notice that when things don't come together for me, it is usually for the best. God guides you through life. When I keep trying to make something happen that just doesn't work, that is God saying, "Don't go that way." I am always glad when I listen and change direction.

There is a Seneca quote I like: "It is not because things are difficult that we do not dare; it is because we do not dare that they are difficult." Dare to know God. Conduct an experiment for a couple of weeks: pay attention, wonder at nature, feel the pulsations of energy in your body, and know that with every breath, you are taking in the life force that sustains you. Look for how life comes together for you. When things don't work out, did you change course and discover it was for the best?

Belief is not very powerful; knowledge and experience are. If you just believe in something, it is a concept. It might or might not be true. When you have knowledge of something, and directly experience it, no one can take that away from you.

If you get hung up on the word God, substitute Source, Energy, Prana, Shakti, Spirit, Buddha Nature, Higher Consciousness, Christ Consciousness, Pure Presence, Higher Self, The Witness, The Now... don't let the name keep you from the experience.

To remind you that witnessing is not just observing, but also connecting to God, I will capitalize Witness throughout the rest of this book.

CONNECT TO THE WITNESS
RATHER THAN JUST WITNESS

Witnessing is more than just watching thoughts and feelings. It is connecting to the presence that watches. It is connecting to pure awareness, the blank canvas where thoughts and forms appear and disappear. When you connect to the Witness, it is like watching yourself as a character in a movie called Life.

A movie where nothing ever happens to the characters would be a bore to watch. The movies that you like best are the ones where the characters go through the joys and tribulations of life, where there is drama, mystery, and excitement. The reason you enjoy these movies is that, as you watch, you know you are not really those characters going through all that drama.

When you connect to the Witness, you can enjoy the *Life* movie in which you've been cast. You are disengaged from the drama and excitement because you realize you are the one who watches, rather than the character in the drama. You connect to the source that you are, and just like watching a good movie, you enjoy the experience of life.

As you connect to the Witness and dispassionately watch everything that arises, you become the center of the storm, stable and peaceful. Ironically, in the dispassion, you feel more alive and joyful, because you are fully experiencing life.

Passion is a mental state of excitement, even though we tend to mistake it for a feeling from the heart. The love from the heart has a peace and spaciousness to it, which allows you to engage fully in life. The excitement from the mind has a grasping quality to it, which clouds your judgment. When you connect to the Witness, you become aware of the spacious unchanging presence that is undisturbed regardless of whether the mind likes something or dislikes it. You connect to a source that notices all the contents of your life, your thoughts, words, actions, and situations.

I've talked to many people who claim to Witness their thoughts, but they are really just stuck in mental and verbal complaining. They notice they are unhappy, but they are not disengaged and watching the unhappiness from the distance of the Witness. When you complain, you avoid the experience of being with discomfort. You notice you are miserable. Instead of experiencing misery, you talk about it. *About* is not the experience of *it*. Being aware that you are unhappy, and connecting to the awareness itself, are completely different experiences.

When you only watch yourself complain or dislike a situation, nothing gets resolved. Connect to the Witness by noticing that you are watching. You have to actually connect to the one who watches. You are not your discomfort, fear, sadness, or anger, because you can watch these emotions and feelings. This will allow you to stay with the experience so it can move through you. When you connect, the experience is not as bad as your dramatic mind has made it out to be. You see how it really is, and can find a solution based in reality, not fantasy.

When you notice you are miserable, connect to the part of you that notices this. Shift into watching your discomfort from the perspective of watching a character in a movie; be *aware* that you are watching. As you connect to this awareness notice how misery feels in your body. What does your chest feel like, your belly, and throat?

Breathe deeply to help you allow the sensations to exist as they are. As you stay with the Witness, you create space to feel what is before you, and the misery will dissipate. You will gain clarity about yourself and the situation. Just like when you watch a movie, you clearly see what the character should do next.

WITHDRAW TO CONNECT

There is a practice in yoga called *pratyahara*. It literally means withdrawing from the senses. Your senses bring in information through touch, taste, sound, sight, and smell. Your mind decides that you like or dislike this information. *Pratyahara* is withdrawing your attention from the judgments, opinions, and stories the mind creates about the information.

Our self-image is fueled by the mind, through what we think about ourselves. When you identify with your thoughts, judgments, and opinions, you identify with your ego or self-image. You forget that you are the silent source behind all these thought forms. You forget that you are an embodied spirit, a human being.

Most of your thoughts are ego-based and they feed your self-image. A simple way to dis-identify with your ego and connect to your being is to withdraw your attention from the thoughts and stories in your mind. They will still be there of course, but you stop feeding them with energy. They get much quieter, eventually becoming like thought bubbles, or clouds floating through the sky.

As you withdraw your attention from ego-mind consciousness and place it on Witnessing, breathing, and feeling, you connect to your true source. You retain your self-image yet you are not hooked into it. Your true self, the soul within, becomes dominant.

There is nothing wrong with having an ego; it allows us to function in the world. Everyone has an ego. Our problems stem from identifying with our ego or self-image. We forget we are the soul or embodied spirit, and act as if we are our ego, which is always grasping at survival, no matter how much we have. We could have millions of dollars. The ego will convince us that is not enough. We could have one nice house, and the ego will need two or three. No matter what our salary is, it is not enough. The ego is only temporarily satisfied.

Your spirit is so powerful, so abundant, never lacking anything, that when you plug into who you really are, there is no suffering, no lack. Use ego to appropriately function in the world, but all along, know who you really are. Withdraw attention from your mental thoughts and stories to connect to the One behind your thoughts.

This practice of *pratyahara*, or withdrawing from ego-mind, helped me immensely during a training program where I worked in the kitchen of a yoga *ashram*. During this ten-day program, I helped prepare food for eighty people. The days started at 5:30 am and ended at 9:00 or 10:00 pm. I washed dishes, cleaned, and prepared food the entire time. My body would get achy and tired. My mind would complain and make judgments.

I withdrew my attention from those thoughts, focusing on my breath, especially the pause at the top and bottom of the inhalation and exhalation. I dropped the mental story, felt the pure physical sensations in my body, and connected to my breath. My mind would balk, complaining, "OMG! I have eight more days of this, seven more days…" I withdrew my attention, placing it on my breath, pure bodily sensation, and the Witness, over, and over.

The complaining thoughts drained me. When I withdrew from them, I had more energy. The constant withdrawing every time those thoughts and judgments arose connected me to my being, connected me to energy, to the Witness. I often felt joyful when I connected to the Witness and disconnected from my ego thoughts. The ten days went by quickly. Although I was still physically tired, I was not mentally or emotionally tired. I more fully realized the insubstantial nature of my thoughts and opinions. By not feeding them with the energy of my attention, I was more often able to serve joyfully in the kitchen.

Chapter 2

Sensations

TWO TYPES OF SENSATION

There are two types of sensation: emotional and biological. Some possible emotional sensations are anger, sadness, happiness, and fear. They are thought-induced, caused by suppressing past experiences. Those emotional sensations arise in the present when something triggers them. Depending on each person's past, the same situation or event can make one person feel neutral, and another feel angry.

Whether you avoid how you feel, or try to get more of a good feeling, you are hooked—at the mercy of your emotions. It is as though they have a life of their own. You become consumed with anger, guilt, passion, sadness, or happiness.

The problem with the positive emotions is that you fear their opposite. Because you assume some external thing has caused your positive emotion, you have to manage and control situations and circumstances in an attempt to maintain the positive emotion. If you lose the external person or situation, you lose the positive emotion. Since everything always changes, it is impossible to maintain a positive emotion through external efforts.

It is your fear of sadness or anger that keeps you running after happiness or joy. Those emotional sensations that you fight, avoid, or run toward, are the very sensations you need to relax with and accept. The very door you are trying to shut is the door you need to enter. As you practice relaxing and accepting emotional sensations, you pass through them, entering the biological sensations.

Biological sensations are without labels. They are the pure sensations of energy made manifest. They are the language the body uses to communicate to you through sensations of heartbeat, heat, cold, tingles, pulsations, fatigue, constriction, expansion, and pain. They do not have a story as in "I'm so hot, this is miserable!" It is just hot as in temperature. There is no judgment of dislike or like. It is simply the body communicating heat or pain to you—nothing more, nothing less. No story.

The mind makes up the stories to go with the biological sensations. "My back is killing me! I'm never going to get better so I can do the things I used to do... ." The story increases the sensations while keeping you from the pure experience. It keeps you in your head, so you avoid your body, increasing the emotional sensation along with the physical pain.

The biological sensations are the ones that are most helpful in anchoring the mind in the present moment. They can reduce your suffering, even if the body is communicating pain. Closer to reality, they are less intense than emotions. You can more easily feel biological sensations in neutral situations because these sensations are not emotionally charged.

As you consciously connect to biological sensations, you become less emotional. You begin to realize you are not your emotions. The happiness, joy, and peace that you want come from a source within you. You are not dependent on other people or external circumstances to feel joyful and peaceful.

FEELING YOUR SENSATIONS

Another core yoga technique is feeling the physical, biological sensations in the body. When you feel the pure sensations, you are in the present moment. When that moment is unpleasant, practice feeling with the Witness. Since sensations are physical, they give you something concrete to focus on, taking you out of "worry" mind and your mental filter, into the direct experience.

Thoughts affect sensations in the body, and the body can affect thoughts. If you are peaceful, but suddenly stub your toe, your mind becomes agitated and your thoughts are probably negative. Perhaps your body is calm, but you are sitting in your living room worried about finances, or you think of something bad that happened in your past. Soon your body feels hot, your belly has a knot, and your heart rate increases.

When you go into the body and feel the pure sensations, you remove, or at least reduce, the mental suffering. This usually reduces the uncomfortable sensations in the body. If sensations are the result of mental worry, then most of the suffering will subside. If sensations are due to illness or injury, the discomfort subsides, but may not completely disappear.

Thoughts about discomfort increase the discomfort. When you Witness your thoughts and take the drama out of them, feeling the pure sensation beneath the mental opinions, you greatly reduce your suffering. As you observe yourself feeling sensations, you know you cannot possibly be the sensations. You are the one who experiences them.

The ego-mind is very tricky and can fool us. The body is not capable of lying, so whenever you want to know what you really think, pay attention to your body. If you are angry, scared, or happy, you and everyone else can see it on your face and posture. Maybe you have experienced someone telling you something and you know he or she is lying. This is probably because you see the truth in their body. Someone tells you he is relaxed, that everything is just fine. Yet you can see the tension etched on his face and in his posture. His tone of voice is slightly harsh.

Our body always communicates with us in the form of sensations. When you connect to sensations you connect to your body, and to what you truly think about a situation. What you feel does not mean it is the ultimate truth about a circumstance; it just tells you what you personally feel about it. Someone else might feel differently about the same situation.

LET GO OF YOUR PAST

Feeling sensations gives you the opportunity to let go of your past and live life now, as it is. Often when something traumatic happens, you can't handle it. For good reason, you escape by pushing it into the subconscious. This is especially the case when you are a child, with limited understanding. This escape causes the trauma to become an undercurrent in your life. The fear and trauma that you "escaped" from will seep into your relationships, your finances, and your health. Your body and psyche do not forget what your mind has pushed away.

One day I showed a woman to a cabin she was to share with several other women during a retreat. It was a nice cabin, not far from the road, near a small wooded area and a lake. As we approached the cabin, she became agitated. Before I even got the door open, she turned to me, saying, "I have to get out of here!" I was surprised, since it was such a peaceful, pretty environment. As we left, she calmed down and told me that years ago a man attacked her in the woods. As a result, she just cannot be anywhere near the woods.

Because she couldn't allow herself to experience the attack at the time, the event continues to resurface. Life does not allow you to avoid anything, not even trauma. She will continue to have opportunities to experience her past until she faces it and feels it, which will release it. It is not easy to face past trauma, which is why it is essential to connect to the Witness when experiencing your past in the present.

The body holds memory, even when your conscious mind forgets. You do not need to know why you have fear and anxiety in order to experience it. Understanding why can take a long time, and can be just another form of escape or avoidance. To release yourself from the past, simply Witness, and breathe deeply with the surfacing sensations.

The depth of the trauma determines the amount of support you might need now. You might not be able to Witness, feel, and breathe on your own. If the sensations are extreme, you might need a teacher, therapist, counselor, or psychiatrist to support you while you Witness the fear and anxiety. Experiencing the past in the present is not easy, but the freedom is worth it.

Any situation can be interpreted by the mind as traumatic, and affect your life. I remember quietly working on an assignment in second-grade math class when suddenly the teacher got very mad at one of the students. Although I did not know what he did to upset her, I do remember what the teacher did. She yanked the boy out of his chair and put him in the corner of the room. She repeatedly hit him with a ruler as she yelled at him.

Although the teacher only intended to punish the boy, she unknowingly punished me too. I was terrified that if she did that to him, maybe I would be next. Since I wasn't aware of what the boy did to cause her anger, it seemed to me like it happened for no reason. I didn't understand what was going on. I was scared, and "escaped" from the discomfort.

I remember holding my breath, trying to make myself invisible throughout most of her class that year. I have struggled in math ever since. All through grade school when I had to do math I could feel myself shut down because I would be so uncomfortable. I worked hard, struggling to make Cs in all my years of math classes. Emotionally I felt like that second-grader trying to make herself invisible so as not to be beaten.

When you cannot experience something when it happens, regardless of the reason, it will continue to bubble up. When you experience it in the safer environment of the present, you release it, and regain your freedom to enjoy life. Even experiencing only a small part of your past will give you some relief, and the strength, to experience and release more next time.

Experiencing this temporary discomfort is not pleasant. Neither is the undercurrent of fear or anger and the effect they are having in your life. It is better to go through the discomfort and be released from your prison of fear. This practice of connecting to the Witness, bodily sensations, and breath, will help you experience whatever arises, releasing you from it. As pain and suffering move out, you make room for peace and joy to emerge.

PRACTICE WITH SENSATIONS

Getting in touch with pure biological sensations is easiest, during, and immediately after, physical activity. These sensations are pleasant. There is no emotion involved, so it is easy to stay with them.

Try the following exercise:

Jump around, run in place, or vigorously clap your hands for a moment. When you stop, close your eyes and feel the tingles and pulsations in your body. They are strongest in the arms and hands because of all the nerve endings there. Feel the pulsating energy coursing through your veins. At first, these sensations might be subtle. With practice, you increase your sensitivity and they become stronger.

As you focus your attention, you will notice the sensations increase. Continued practice of this exercise will increase your sensitivity. At some point, you will be able to feel this energy pulsating without doing physical activity. As you read a book, or relax in a chair, bring your attention to your arms and hands. Feel the sensations there. Eventually you will feel them everywhere, even in the legs and feet.

Energy follows your attention and your attention increases energy. To demonstrate this, shake out your arms and clap your hands several times. Then be still. Feel the pulsations and tingles in your arms and hands. Now, place all of your attention into your right arm and hand only. Just your right arm and hand. What did you notice about your left arm and hand? It all but disappeared, didn't it?

The right arm, where you placed your attention, was throbbing with sensation and energy while the arm that received no attention disappeared. What else do you feed with energy by giving it your attention? When you don't know, you are creating your life from unconsciousness. The Witness shows you what you feed with your thoughts and attention.

Once you can feel the sensations in the above exercises, practice feeling sensations with slightly irritating situations, ones that cause mild to moderate reactions. For me, this can be domestic chores or driving in traffic. The busier I am, the more I have to do, the greater my resistance to the chore. There are times I work all day at my job, teach yoga in the evening, come home to cook dinner, and then have to wash the dishes. I notice I'm tired. I don't want to wash the dishes. So there I am at the sink, banging pots and pans, mentally complaining. There is a feeling of tightness in my chest and tension in my muscles. My breathing is shallow and, in general, I feel uncomfortable since I don't want to do what I am doing.

Observing this resistance to what I am doing helps provide some detachment, allowing me to practice relaxing. I Witness my negative thoughts from a distance, as though I'm watching a frustrated character in a movie. As I feel the sensations of my hands in the soapy warm water, the pressure of wiping the sponge against the pots, the ache in my legs, the frustration begins to dissipate. I deepen my breath, and I begin to relax. I feel my feet connect with the floor; my ribs expand and contract with my deeper breathing. I Witness my thoughts changing from negative to neutral, or at least receding to the background.

If I need an extra boost, I add the gratefulness practice. How wonderful it is to have two strong legs even if they are achy. I'm so glad I have indoor plumbing and electricity to make washing dishes easy. Now I notice the feeling of my muscles releasing, my chest relaxing as the tightness dissolves. My legs still ache, yet I don't mind so much. This chore of washing dishes is not so bad after all, as I return to the reality of just washing dishes.

When someone cuts me off in traffic, it usually triggers a reaction in me. I feel some strong, unpleasant sensations. Those are usually knots in my stomach, constriction in my chest and throat, heat throughout my torso and head. I feel the discomfort, and Witness my thoughts and feelings about the situation. I Witness how part of me enjoys being upset and mentally cursing the other driver. I also Witness and feel my discomfort and tension, so I deepen my breath to stay present and relax. Soon I can feel my muscles release. The heat and constriction dissipate. In a very short time I feel much better and more relaxed. I don't even care anymore that I was cut off.

WITNESS AND FEEL

When you practice feeling bodily sensations, it is important to Witness the pure feelings without getting caught in your *thoughts about the feelings.* Often we focus on the like/dislike decisions we make, rather than experiencing the pure sensations in the body. Your mind will label them as good, bad, sad, happy, or scared, spinning a dramatic story around those labels. Just notice that you have attached a label. Then go back to simply feeling the pure physical sensation beneath the thought. It is also important to deepen your breath so you can relax with the sensations and feel them longer. Sometimes sensations can be strong or unpleasant and you will not want to stay with them.

Some people have trouble feeling and experiencing pleasant sensations because they think they don't deserve to feel good. Whatever issues you are dealing with, the practice of feeling and staying present with sensations will free you. You will notice they ebb and flow, eventually dissolving. As they release, so will your fears about what caused the sensations. This practice can help your fears and insecurities slowly melt away.

Your mind will have some strong opinions—likes and dislikes—when you practice feeling sensations. Witness whatever comes up to remove some of the drama about it. Give the feelings and thoughts space to simply exist, without doing anything about it. Just watch it all. Feel it all. Breathe, breathe, and breathe. Remember, the breath is your lifeline, helping you relax, allowing what arises to be what it is.

Watch how what arises comes and goes in the awareness of the Witness. As you practice this, your need to control circumstances will subside, giving you more energy to enjoy your life, rather than avoiding it.

DECISION MAKING WITH SENSATIONS

Since the body is not capable of lying, feeling sensations can be a valuable guide in making decisions. With practice, you can discern whether sensations are coming from a place of reaction or a place of bodily wisdom. If they are from a place of reaction, you need to watch, feel, and breathe, so you can stay with them until you begin to relax.

Reactions are very emotional in nature and create strong, even panicky, sensations. Those subside as you continue being present with them. Sensations coming from wisdom are not so emotional. An example that comes to mind is my decision to take a writing class.

I was in the midst of renovating my house to sell, and preparing to leave my career, when I decided I should take a writing class. I wasn't sure what type of career I would be starting, but I assumed it would involve going back to school. I hadn't done much writing since I graduated from college over twenty years earlier. I figured I had better brush up on some skills. So I checked out the classes being offered, and gathered the registration information for the class I decided to take. Extremely busy with renovating the house, my job, and teaching yoga, I knew I would somehow fit the class into my schedule.

The day before the registration date, I began to feel my stomach knotting up, my chest constricting, and my throat tightening. As registration time grew closer, these sensations increased. I knew I had better listen to my body, so I decided not to take the class. As soon as I made the decision, those sensations all disappeared, replaced with sensations of relief and comfort. My body told me I made the right decision. It was my ego pushing me to take a class regardless of how much I already had on my plate. My body knew I couldn't possibly fit that in while giving the class the attention it would require.

This next example is more emotional and complicated. When I moved to Florida, my life was in major transition, and I didn't know how I would support myself. I had many decisions to make. Should I go back to school? Look for a job in the career for which I was trained? Pursue something in yoga, stress management, or relaxation? There were many possibilities, which created confusion.

My parents wanted me to go back to school because they thought that would lead to a guaranteed job. My mind liked that idea too, because it seemed safe. My heart and body told me to pursue a career in yoga and write a book. My mind was worried I wouldn't be able to support myself with yoga, and that I didn't know how to pursue that kind of a career.

I had much doubt about what to do, how to do it, and a lot of input from other people, which further confused the decision. It was also trickier than the writing class decision, because this was more emotional, with my fears creating sensations.

I would use my practice to get calm and centered. Then I imagined going back to school or the career I just left, and felt constriction in my chest, a knot in my belly, and a general sinking sensation. When I thought about teaching stress-management, relaxation, and yoga, I felt calm, expansive, free, and relaxed.

With this emotional decision, it was important that I be calm and centered. In that space, I could trust the sensations in my body because they came from wisdom. When I was not centered, they came from fear and ego, which was misleading. As I moved forward with teaching yoga, I noticed what support I received from life. I also continued to check in with my bodily sensations periodically so I would know if I needed to adjust my plans.

CHOOSING NOT TO REACT

When you Witness the sensations you feel, you give yourself choices. You do not have to succumb to those sensations. You can Witness your sensations become stronger, and feel yourself about to react before it happens. This gives you time to take action instead. Using this technique helped me at a time when my father was in the hospital and the doctors were not sure if he would live.

I was in my sister's home, taking care of my two-year-old niece, who wanted to play. At the same time I was trying to entertain her, the dog was panicking about a coming thunderstorm. While I juggled caring for my niece and the dog, I worried about my dad. I could feel the sensations in my body become more and more uncomfortable, as I felt overwhelmed. The Witness gave me the detachment to see what was happening at the same time I experienced it. I could Witness myself feel hot, my chest become constricted, and the sensations of mounting pressure. I knew I was headed for a meltdown if I didn't remove myself from the situation.

I chose to do so.

I put my niece in the car seat and drove to the grocery store. She was happy being wheeled around in the cart, playing with my car keys. The grocery shopping gave me something physical to concentrate on, keeping my mind off my dad. I would feel the sensations of reaching for the can of beans and placing it in the cart. Next, I reached for the bag of rice. I felt my hand on the cart as I pushed it down the aisles, my feet making contact with the floor, the feel of my breath moving in and out.

By the time we were ready to check out, I felt much better. Even the rain that now poured down didn't bother me. My niece and I shared a wonderful moment, watching the storm while we ate the ice cream I had bought. When I got back to the house, I was able to comfort the dog.

Accepting the reality of your situation does not mean you cannot change it. In fact, you have to accept it first, in order to change it, because acceptance gives you the clarity to make another choice. Through the awareness of noticing where I was, I could choose a different experience by choosing to change the situation. **You create your life.** Once you accept what is before you, you can create something different if you so choose. Often we don't accept; instead, we complain, resist, wish it were different... so we lose our power to create something else.

CHANGE SENSATIONS
THROUGH ACTIVITY

You can also work with sensations by replacing negative feelings with positive feelings through activity. It is difficult to be sad when you sing, play an instrument, or do anything you find fun, with other people who are also having fun.

When I moved from North Carolina to Florida, there were many unknowns in my life. I did not have a job, or much money. Recently separated from my husband, I had no social life. This was an easy situation for my thoughts to spiral downward, to cause me to feel sad and anxious.

At one low point, I got on the Internet and found a group of people that met nearby for drumming. The first thirty minutes was a lesson, followed by an hour of drumming. This was perfect since I didn't know how to drum. Surrounded by people making rhythms and having fun together, I soon pulled out of my depression. By the time I got back home, I felt really good. I also sang with a church choir for several months during this time. I always felt better singing with others who were enjoying themselves. Plus, you can't hold your breath while singing!

Perhaps sports, arts, or crafts are what help you enjoy life. It is important to have something that can uplift you when you find yourself in a downward spiral. Know that this activity is not intended as an escape. If you do something to avoid what you are feeling, you are not using it consciously to help yourself. If you depend on the activity to provide relief, then you are escaping. When you stay with the practice of Witnessing and feeling sensations, the activity can be an uplifting experience used to break a negative cycle.

Use the body to replace negative feelings through posture. If you feel down, smile. Force a laugh, and it will soon turn into real laughter. My sister and I did this when we were kids. We would be laughing hysterically for a good thirty minutes or more. I still do it occasionally, even as an adult. It feels so good! These activities work well if you are just a little sad or down.

When immersed in deep negativity or depression, it is very hard to make yourself smile or laugh. When I am beyond that effort, I find it helpful to roll my shoulders back and down, to open my chest and heart. Try clasping your hands behind your head, with the elbows extending out to the sides and slightly up. Gently lift your chin. Take some deep breaths. These techniques are very simple, and may help you feel better.

CONSCIOUSNESS AND ENERGY

As you practice connecting to the sensations of energy in your body, and to the Witness, you are getting in touch with your divine nature.

Everything in physical existence is made of energy. Einstein proved this with his formula $E = mc^2$. Science continues to verify this. Something comes into your consciousness, you expend energy through your actions to create it, and the created form consists of atoms of energy vibrating to a particular frequency.

Energy is the clay, or medium, through which consciousness creates the forms that make up life. When you connect to the Witness, you connect to pure un-manifested consciousness. Remember the blank canvas analogy? When you bring your attention to felt sensations, you connect to the energy through which consciousness manifests.

When you are in the presence of consciousness and energy, you are in the present moment, connected to your true self. As you withdraw your attention from ego-mind thoughts and feelings, placing your attention on the Witness and pure sensations, who you *are not* begins to recede so *who you are* can emerge.

Your true self is peaceful and relaxed in every situation. It is always present, covered up by who you are not, by your self-image. As you focus your attention on consciousness and energy, the covering of your self-image becomes thinner, and the loving presence that you are shines forth more and more. While you still have a self-image, you become its master, not its slave.

Chapter 3

Breath

THE MAIN CARRIER OF ENERGY

Breath is not just air. Without it, there is no life, since breath is the main vehicle for carrying the life force energy into your body.

You also receive energy from food. It is possible to live about a month without food. Without the energy from breath, you will only live minutes.

It is this energy that animates your body and gives thoughts to your mind. Energy is invisible, yet it supports everything that lives. When you consciously connect to the breath, you connect to the energy of life itself.

Because you can consciously control your breath, you can use it to change your body and mind. You can use breath to melt away tension and free the mind of worry, returning to the state of relaxation. When you deepen and slow down your breath, your mind will also slow down. Your body will begin to relax.

When stressed, you are tense. Your breath is high and shallow in the chest. You are not connected to life when using this unconscious breath, which is why you feel tired, or even exhausted. There is very little energy coming into your body. The little that does is consumed by your frantic, anxious thoughts. The following breathing techniques help to slow and deepen the breath, and reconnect you to life.

EXTENDED EXHALATIONS

Begin this breathing technique by noticing your natural breath. Feel the cool air pass through the nostrils as you inhale, warmer air pass through as you exhale. Feel the chest gently rise and fall with the breath. Notice if the breath is shallow or deep. Relax, as you watch the natural rhythm of your breath. If opinions or judgments about your natural breath arise, notice them. Then return to watching and breathing. After a moment of noticing the breath, count the length of the natural inhale, and the length of the natural exhale. Once you have established the count, begin to lengthen your exhalations. If you counted two on your inhale, lengthen your exhale to three or four.

It is important not to struggle with this. Do not create tension in the name of relaxation! If a count of four creates tension, back off to three or two. Even inhalations and exhalations are fine if extended exhalations cause tension. The eventual goal is to exhale twice as long as you inhale. You might need to work up to that. You will notice the inhalation automatically lengthens too, but stay focused on the exhalation in this technique. Once you are used to it, you will not need to count; you can simply lengthen your exhalation by feel.

If you get too goal-oriented and create tension, go back to normal breathing, and feel the sensations of the normal breath. Once you feel relaxed, try to lengthen the exhalation again. When first attempting this, practice under neutral circumstances. Practice in bed before falling asleep, or before getting up in the morning. Another good time is when you walk; inhale for two steps, exhale for four steps. Adjust the count and pace of walking as needed. Maybe inhale for one step, exhale two steps. If you are walking fast, inhale five and exhale ten. Do whatever you can without causing tension.

Practice this technique when you stand in line or wait at a traffic light. Practice as you wash the dishes, or while folding laundry. Once you have the hang of long exhalations, try it when you are in a slightly uncomfortable situation. As you practice, it will not take long for it to feel natural. Whenever you feel tense, you will automatically turn to your deep breath to undo the tension and relax. As you deepen your exhale, you slow the mind and relax the body, returning yourself to the state of relaxation.

BELLY BREATHING AND FULL BREATHING

A second helpful breathing technique is belly breathing, followed by full breathing. Watch babies and small children breathe. Notice that their bellies rise and fall with the breath. Yours did too, when you were little, because that is the natural way to breathe. Although this technique is called belly breathing, you are not really breathing into the belly. You are using your diaphragm muscle, which causes the belly to rise and fall.

Initiating the breath from the diaphragm engages the parasympathetic nervous system, which creates the relaxation response. This system also regulates digestion, heart rate, and blood pressure. It maintains the breath when you are asleep or unconscious. When you take conscious, full breaths, engaging the diaphragm, you are affecting a system you normally have no control over. You are able to effect a positive change on your digestion and blood pressure by engaging the parasympathetic nervous system through this breathing technique.

When the breath is tense and high in the chest, you engage the sympathetic nervous system, which regulates the fight or flight response. This response is useful if your life is really in danger and you need to survive. In our stress-filled lives, this system remains activated constantly. This state of high alert causes chronic stress and health problems.

When you breathe from the belly, you activate the relaxation response and the parasympathetic nervous system. It is impossible to be relaxed and stressed out at the same time, so belly breathing gives you time to recover from fight or flight.

The diaphragm muscle attaches to the bottom ribs, and separates the belly from the ribcage. When you inhale, the diaphragm moves down toward the belly, opening the lungs. When you exhale, it moves up toward the lungs and expels the breath. This method fills the lungs from the bottom up, like filling a glass of water. It makes a more efficient and effective breath.

BELLY BREATHING TECHNIQUE

The following is the technique for belly breathing. It is best to learn this lying down. Once you are familiar with it, you can do this sitting, lying down, or standing. Since we lie down when going to sleep, I recommend practicing this in bed before falling asleep, and again before getting up.

- Lie down comfortably.
- Place one palm on your upper belly just under the ribcage, above the navel.
- Relax a moment with normal breathing.
- When you are ready, as you exhale, gently press your belly down with your palm. Just press it down a little. Do not create tension.

- As you inhale, relax your hand, and feel the belly rise with the inhale.

- Every time you exhale, press the belly down gently.

- Inhale and allow the belly to rise.

- Breathe this way as long as it feels comfortable. At any point, if you feel stressed, take normal breaths.

After you are familiar with this breath, you will not need to keep your palm on the belly. Relax both arms near your sides, and continue belly breathing. With practice, this will once again become your normal breath. Soon, every time you breathe, it will be with the diaphragm. Just relax, and allow the belly to rise and fall with the breath.

Do not force this. Remember, this is the natural breath you used as a child. Your body remembers how to do it, so relax your mind. Let your body do what it knows how to do. It might help as you inhale, to visualize your breath traveling toward your belly, causing it to rise like a balloon. Think of the exhalation as deflating the balloon. If frustration or tension arises, notice that, and return to your normal breath. When you feel relaxed, resume the technique.

FULL BREATHING TECHNIQUE

Once you are comfortable with belly breathing, it is time to add full breathing. Do not practice full breathing until belly breathing becomes natural. At first, practice full breathing

❖

while lying down with knees bent and feet on the floor, or while lying in bed. If you are comfortable with your legs extended out along the floor that is fine.

- Exhale, and feel the belly release down.

- As you inhale, feel the belly rise. Continue to inhale as you notice the lower chest, and then the upper chest, rise.

- Once the chest begins to rise, the belly will naturally drop down.

- It helps to think of a wave, one continuous long wave of breath. The wave begins at the belly, rises up, and crests at the top of the chest.

- As you exhale, feel the wave wash into shore—the chest releasing down, and the belly relaxing even more. The body releases down, sinking toward the support beneath you.

It can be helpful to place one palm on the upper belly, beneath the rib cage, and the other palm on the upper chest, beneath the collarbone. Breathe into the bottom hand, and then into the top hand. As you exhale, and feel the top hand release, the bottom hand releases a little more. Relax, as you allow your body to rise and fall on the wave of your breath. Think of it as one continuous wave that begins at the bottom and crests at the top, rather than as part one, part two. You are filling the lungs from the bottom up, belly followed by chest.

You can have a friend watch you if you are not sure you have the technique. Remember, this is going back to your natural breath, so if you simply relax, the breath will naturally do this with just a little guidance from you. If you try too hard you create tension and that makes the technique difficult.

This breath brings maximum oxygen and energy into the body, since the lungs fill entirely. At some point, these techniques will become automatic. You will be able to do them when you stand, walk, or sit. In the beginning, learn them lying down. Soon you will be breathing with your diaphragm all the time.

ANXIETY

If you have anxiety, and find breathing techniques are making it worse, I recommend working with extended exhalations while walking. This takes the focus off the lungs and the breathing, putting it on the walking or the belly.

While you walk, practice even breathing. Inhaling for two steps, exhaling for two steps. Experiment. Adjust the count and pace of your steps as needed, so you do not create tension. Focus your attention on walking and counting, more than on the sensations of breathing. Feel your feet make contact with the floor or ground. By focusing on the walking, you can reduce your anxiety about the breathing, while receiving the benefits of deeper breaths.

Another good technique is the belly breathing described earlier. By focusing only on the belly, you take the mind off the chest and lungs, which can reduce your anxiety around breathing. As you work with these two techniques, you will relax more, and soon be able to incorporate the other breathing techniques. Do not create tension with the breath. If you are getting tense, take normal breaths until the tension dissolves, then try the technique again for a moment.

When you are aware of your breath, you are in the present moment, connected to the energy that supports life. Your breath is your lifeline. Bringing awareness to it immediately helps you relax and calm your mind. It is an instant antidote to fear, anxiety, anger, or any other emotion.

Chapter 4

The Wave of Sensation

THE WAVE

All sensations come and go like waves. Something triggers a reaction; you immediately feel sensation. The intensity builds, the wave comes to a crest, subsides on the downside, and you experience release and resolution. When you allow yourself to feel your experience and ride the wave, you accept life as it is. You experience the flow of life.

Most of the time you don't ride the wave of sensations, so you don't experience flow, or come to creative insight and solutions at the end of an experience. You are triggered constantly, reacting again and again. You might find temporary release, but situations continue to upset you because the experience isn't resolved. In place of finding peace in your life, you find conflict.

By staying with the wave of sensation, you take advantage of an opportunity to resolve your reactions and be free of them.

You react to life less often as you ride the waves of sensation. If a situation needs to change, you arrive at a creative solution for permanent change when you go through this process.

Here is a diagram of the sensation wave with further explanation:

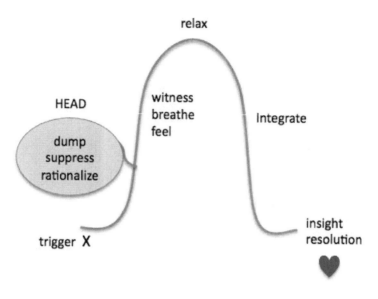

© Kamini Desai

The wave begins with a trigger. This is something that causes you to react, such as a driver cutting you off in traffic, someone insulting you, or your partner leaving you. Sensations arise almost immediately after the trigger, so fast it can feel simultaneous. You don't want to feel these sensations, so you jump off the wave to avoid them.

Jumping off the wave can happen in three ways: when you **dump, suppress** or **rationalize**. You move into your head and this keeps you from feeling the sensation of the wave. When you dump, you are acting out or reacting. Typically, this is in the form of mental or verbal complaining, rolling the eyes, or smirking. Sometimes it involves throwing things, hitting a pillow, or even another person.

The dumping feels good in the moment, and maybe immediately afterward, as it provides a temporary release. However, it resolves nothing. You likely made more trouble for yourself and others. Depending on how you reacted, you might now be in a cycle of guilt or remorse.

The second way to avoid unpleasant sensations is to suppress. That's when you push your feelings down, paste on a smile, proclaiming that you are just fine. After a while, you even believe this. You might become a martyr, and think suppressing is a good thing. The body isn't capable of lying though, so your "fineness" will bubble up in the form of tight shoulders, back pain, controlled and rigid movements, or even illness.

The third way to jump off the wave is by rationalizing. This is when you tell yourself and others, "I am right." Someone just did something rude or outrageous to you and now you are very rightly angry. You exclaim to your friend, "Can you believe what Nancy just did?" Your friend, of course, agrees with you, further confirming that you are right.

It does not matter if you are right or not, what matters is that you have justified not feeling the sensations.

When you rationalize, you decide that what happened should not have happened. The truth is it did. You now are in a fight with reality, missing the opportunity to get at the root of your reactions and resolve them for good.

Rationalization hooks us more than dumping or suppression. When you are "right," it is easier to stay off the wave. It becomes extremely challenging to get back on. Remember, the point is not about being right. It is about staying on the wave of sensation. If you truly are right, at the end of the wave you will gain the insight to skillfully adjust the situation.

If the wave is intense, it can help to jump off in a less reactive way, and return to experiencing the wave after a break. I like to go for a run or hit tennis balls on a backboard. Someone told me they put an icepack on the back and side of their neck to "cool off" for immediate relief. Once you have released a little, you can get back on the wave and stay on longer. Depending on the size of the wave, you might need to jump off and on several times. Each time you are able to stay longer, until you can ride it out to the release and resolution phase.

When you are triggered, your reaction to something or someone is an unresolved issue in the subconscious coming up. When you stay with the pure wave of sensations, you allow release and resolution to happen. This is the way you break reactive patterns, and live more in the present moment, relaxing with life. You do not need to understand where your reactions come from or why you have them. You just need to experience them.

HOW TO RIDE THE WAVE

To help you stay on the wave, engage the practice of Witnessing, breathing, and feeling pure sensations beneath the mental labels. Staying with the wave is the process of moving from thinking and living in your head, to feeling and living in your heart. Connecting to the Witness helps you disengage from the intensity of the thoughts and feelings as they arise on the wave. The breath helps you to relax with your experience. Feeling the sensations allows the energy to flow. This combination of techniques breaks the long-held reactive patterns, enabling you to relax with more people and circumstances.

Through the entire process, continue to watch, feel, and breathe, becoming more integrated and relaxed. As the sensation wave dissipates, you reach a place of insight. Often you discover there is nothing you need to do, because you have internally resolved your issue. You are at peace.

When you align with reality, the situation takes care of itself. Whatever triggered you doesn't bother you anymore. It is a non-issue because you feel peaceful.

Sometimes it is still necessary to adjust an external situation. If that is the case, your action will be appropriate to the situation, because it comes from direct experience and insight, rather than from avoidance and reaction. The solution will be creative, resolving the circumstance. In riding the wave to completion, you don't react to life, you respond to life.

Using these techniques to stay on the wave helps keep the mind from getting dramatic and spinning stories. Your thoughts about an experience are much more uncomfortable than the actual experience. Even the worst reality is more kind than your imagination. The worst reality has an end, whereas your thoughts about something keep it alive for the rest of your life.

Riding the wave of sensation is the process of accepting reality and life as it is, rather than how your mind thinks it should be. This is the process of moving more into your heart, and surrendering to the divine plan.

WHY STAY ON THE WAVE

When you resist life, sensations and energy become blocked in your body and psyche. You are not able to reach the release and resolution on the downside of the wave. When you avoid what is uncomfortable you do not escape it. It submerges into the subconscious and affects your life from there. You unconsciously attract the "wrong" partners. No matter what you do, you can't make much money. Success is only achieved through hard work, or whatever other story you unconsciously create.

When beliefs become lodged in the subconscious, you are helpless to make changes, because they are hidden. Only when they rise into your consciousness, can you release your habits and beliefs, to create different experiences for yourself. Feeling the sensations of your experience from the viewpoint of the Witness, and accepting what is there, brings the hidden patterns to light, releasing them.

When you accept reality, rather than resist it, you can be at peace with your life. You will have the insight to make changes if necessary. **Accepting is not the same thing as liking, it is allowing, and recognizing reality as it is.** You can accept your dislike of a situation by allowing yourself to experience dislike.

When you accept your experience, you can take action to bring about a change from a place of peace, as opposed to one of conflict. When you wish something were different, you are in denial of reality, and in conflict. When you deny reality, your action to make a change is usually ineffective because your reality is based on conflict, and on what you wish were real, ignoring what is true.

When you stay on the wave of sensation through completion, you can fully experience the situation and resolve the internal issues that caused your reaction in the first place. You move into a space of insight and clarity as the wave dissipates.

For example, when I became the manager of a kitchen at a yoga *ashram*, the hours were brutally long. I was in a constant state of exhaustion. The volunteers that came and went were exhausted too, which made it difficult to keep the kitchen staffed.

I accepted the situation by allowing myself to experience it, using my practice to stay with the sensations of fifteen-hour days in the kitchen. I repeatedly applied the practice of Witnessing, feeling, and breathing, with whatever sensation waves were arising. I might feel tired, resentful, joyful, grateful, unsure of myself, or angry. Whatever came up, I applied the practice to stay on the wave.

I would experience the downside of the wave, and relax more and more with my experience. The waves became smaller, and further apart. After some months, I came to the downside of the wave cycle for that experience and felt more at peace. Only then did I have insight into how to restructure the kitchen so the workday would be shorter for everyone.

Through the process of accepting, I resolved some of my internal issues of overworking to prove my self-worth. From that internal shift, I was able to create a real solution to an external problem. When your solutions come from a place of internal peace, they create external peace. When solutions come from internal conflict, they create external conflict.

PRACTICE STAYING ON THE WAVE

The bigger the wave of sensation, the harder it is to stay on it. This is why, at first, you practice with circumstances that create only small waves. Just like learning to play a musical instrument, you do not start with performing a concert.

If a large wave crashes over you, the practice is to jump off and back on, repeatedly, until you can ride it out. Since the wave is working with sensations in the body, a good place to begin practicing is with biological sensations. You will know how to practice with sensations created from emotional and psychological triggers, as the process is the same.

In the controlled environment of your yoga mat or living room carpet, go into a simple, but challenging pose, such as Chair Pose. Stand with feet hip-width apart. Extend your arms out in front, parallel to the floor. Bend your knees, as though about to sit in a chair, thighs approaching parallel to the floor. Feel the wave of biological sensation immediately begin as you hold the pose. To stay on the wave, practice watching, feeling, and breathing, with detached awareness. Observe what arises in your mind from the point of view of the Witness.

| Chair Pose partial | Chair Pose full |

As you observe your reactions, your resistance to holding the pose, and your dislike of the building sensations, breathe, and feel the pure biological sensations to stay on the wave. Remain in contact with the physical sensations beneath the mental judgments and comments about them. Stay on your edge; that place where you are not struggling, but are not comfortable. Come out of the pose part way, or all the way, if you enter into struggle.

As you watch yourself, you gain insight. Do you tend to fight the resistance, or do you give up easily? Can you allow the sensations to exist without the need to change them? Can you use the breath to relax with the resistance? With practice you can. Come out of the pose before you enter into struggle.

As soon as you come out of the pose, experience the downside of the sensation wave. Witness feeling the flood of energy in your body—all the tingles, pulsations, and warmth. These sensations might be subtle or barely detectable at first. Just be open, and curious to what might be there for you to feel. If you feel nothing, just Witness the experience of release of effort, of stillness. Witness the relief of letting go.

Notice how the mind changed from aversion to holding the pose, to attraction from releasing the pose. Continue feeling the sensations of release until they dissipate. Perhaps you are in the "no pain no gain" camp, never allowing yourself to experience the release of the downside of the wave.

What you do in the controlled environment of your mat, you do in your life. If you resist stillness and do not allow yourself to receive the benefits of the release, perhaps you have difficulty receiving. For example, you might have a hard time accepting compliments or gifts. If you are restless and want to hurry through poses on the mat, you are likely in a rush all the time.

Because the yoga mat is a controlled environment, and the waves are smaller, you can more easily practice these techniques and see yourself clearly. Experience the wave completely, as you hold and release the pose. Stay connected to the Witness, and the breath, as you feel the pure sensations of the wave. As you do this with poses, the techniques will be more accessible in your life off the mat.

The next place to practice staying on the wave is with situations that only slightly irritate you. Over time, as you practice, you will find you are able to stay with bigger waves.

There will be plenty of times you jump off the wave. When you notice that you have done so, you have the choice of getting back on. As you practice staying on the wave as long as you can, you are building your psychic strength, and next time you can stay on a little longer.

Crises are tsunamis of sensations. It takes a well-established practice to stay on those waves, or to get back on when you jump off. Whatever waves you find yourself on, use the practice to surf. With time, you can stay on longer and be relaxed with more of the reality in your life. Your life will begin to change, as you align with reality, and experience it fully. **You gain clarity and insight to create the life you want, and to be at peace with the life you have.** It is a process of co-creating. Accept what life offers you, learn from it, and skillfully make changes, if that is appropriate.

YOUR REACTIONS ARE A REFLECTION OF YOU

Families and loved ones are often our biggest triggers, which is why relationships can be challenging. When I was forty-two, I ended a fourteen-year career and went through a divorce. I relocated to Florida, moving in with my parents.

When I made that move, I arrived with my insecurities and fears. I worried what I would do with my life, and how to make a living. My family reflected my fear in their comments and questions. It seemed as though everyone was concerned for my future, and gave voice to that.

Everywhere I turned, I was looking in the mirror of fear and doubt. This was a big wave for me. At times, I had to isolate myself by avoiding others, because I just couldn't look in that mirror and face their questions and comments. I would jump off the wave of fear sensations, return, and get back to feeling. The pure feeling of fear, although uncomfortable, was not as bad as the *idea* of the fear.

During this wave of fear, I surrounded myself as much as possible with fellow practitioners who cared about me, yet were not so emotionally involved. This gave me the strength and support to process through my fear of the unknown. As I stayed with this practice, the waves of fear got smaller. They even disappeared for longer periods. I noticed as the fear dissipated, I didn't feel as uncomfortable when family and loved ones asked about my plans or voiced their concerns. I felt more at peace, even though the situation hadn't changed.

Simply understanding where something comes from is of limited value. You need to *feel it,* and *experience it,* so it can come to resolution and disappear. Although it seemed my loss of career, marriage, and home caused my fear, that would not be accurate. The fear was already present, affecting me through my subconscious. Those external circumstances were the trigger, bringing it to the surface. Using the practice to allow myself to feel the pure sensations of fear, minus the label around it, eventually helped move much of it out.

Chapter 5

Formal Practice

MAT WORK

Although the main place to practice all of these techniques is in every moment of your daily life, it is helpful to have a formal practice on your yoga mat. The mat is a controlled environment that allows you to experiment and observe yourself. In life, your environment is not so easily controlled. Anything can happen, at any time, and often does. As you practice within the space of the mat, you get used to using the techniques, and they become more available to you.

A good analogy is playing tennis, or other sports. You practice with drills. You hone your skills in the controlled environment of a ball machine, with a friend or coach, by practicing the different shots and movements over and over. Then, when you play a game against others, you don't think about your shots. You just use them. You don't know what your opponent will do, or what shot you will have to make next, but you are better able to respond because you have practiced. The mat is your practice ground. Just like in sports, no matter how good you get, you always need to practice.

To practice on the mat, put your body in a pose. Choose any pose that causes you some mental irritation and edginess. Chair Pose, or any of the Warrior poses, will work. Or you can just stand tall with your arms extended overhead. After a while, this will create mental reactions and edginess. Once you are in a pose, hold it for a while. Practice watching, feeling, and breathing. Hold the pose on your edge, where your ability to relax intersects with your tendency to react, struggle, or avoid. Feel the energy build, the pure bodily sensations beneath the mental commentary. Witness your mental reaction, the dislike, comments, and judgments that come up, as though you are outside looking in. This will help you detach from the mental drama about the building sensations.

Keep focusing on pure feeling. Deepen your breath to help you relax with the pose. Notice how the mind wants to escape and think of something else. Refocus your attention on the sensations and deep breathing. Stay with yourself through the discomfort. With practice, you discover there is no discomfort, just sensation. Not only with the poses, but also with anything you find stressful. Before you enter into struggle, release the pose. Struggle is when you cannot breathe smoothly, or are unable to relax with the discomfort.

When you release the pose, feel the flood of energy and the sensations coursing through your body. Close your eyes and observe the pleasant feeling. Allow your mind to become absorbed in the sensations. Notice that as you pay attention to the pulsations and tingles of the flooding energy, they grow stronger. After a moment, focus your attention at the center of the forehead, between the eyebrows. This area has a drawing-inward quality to it, a stilling and balancing effect.

If at first, you are not able to feel much sensation after releasing a pose, just focus on the release of effort. As you continue to practice, your ability to feel will increase. Before long, you will start to feel tingles and pulsations of energy. Bring your attention to the release of effort, to the stillness.

As you practice poses in this way, you build your tolerance to stress. Many things that used to bother you will no longer affect you. The practice of watching, feeling, and breathing, will be more available to you in your life because you practice it on your mat. As you practice in your life, it becomes easier to do it on your mat. The two are not separate.

Yoga practice is more than just doing poses to create your own irritation; it is also working with energy. You can feel the energy build, becoming more intense the longer you hold the pose. The irritation you experience is your resistance. You are shining the light of consciousness (Witness) on your resistance. This allows the resistance to soften, and helps you stay with the building energy. Then it simply becomes strong sensations rather than "I don't like it."

When you release the pose, you can feel the energy release, flooding throughout your nerves and body. You can feel the electromagnetic tingles, pulsations, and heat. This flooding energy breaks up your resistance and heals your body. As you practice, your sensitivity will increase. You will be able to feel the energy more strongly, and in areas where at first you could not feel it. Take a moment to focus your attention at the center of the forehead between the eyebrows. Practicing the poses this way gives you access to the healing and protective effects of energy, not just physically in your body, but also mentally and psychologically.

THIRD EYE

The third eye is invisible, which makes it mysterious. It is located at the center of the brain in line with the forehead, between the eyes. Physiologically, the third eye correlates to the pineal gland. The pineal gland secretes melatonin, which *yogis* call *amrita*, the nectar of life. This hormone, in addition to governing the sleep-wake cycle, allowing you to fall asleep, also has many healing properties.

The third eye is your personal pharmacy. When you place your attention at the center of your forehead, the energy of your attention goes all the way back to the brain center and activates the glands there, increasing melatonin production, healing, and restoration.

In addition to its physiologic value, the *yogis* realized that the third eye is a powerful energetic center that balances and integrates energy. It is our connection to spirit, soul, and the cosmic consciousness. Focusing your attention on this site creates a deep stillness, which is helpful for concentration or meditation practice. Whatever focusing or meditation technique you use, if you also place your attention at your third eye, you will experience more stillness. You can even feel your eyes draw slightly back into the sockets as you experience the quality of the energy there.

The third eye is a direct access to your higher consciousness, which is why it is referred to as the eye of insight, or the source of intuition. As you activate this center with your attention, you are in direct communion with your true self, the source of life. When you feel overwhelmed or stressed during the day, bring your attention to the third eye to disengage from who you are not, and to connect with who you are. Connect to the source within you, so you can be *in* the world, not *of* the world.

SITTING PRACTICE

In addition to watching, feeling, and breathing, I find a formal focusing, or sitting, practice very helpful. It is not really a meditation practice, because meditation is a state of being that happens from a prolonged period of concentration. You wouldn't say you practice sleeping. You are either asleep or you are not. You can practice relaxing, which leads to sleep.

The same is true with meditation. You practice concentrating, which can lead to meditation. I find this also takes the pressure off, because if I am practicing meditation, I'm failing most of the time, since I rarely enter that state. I have noticed tremendous benefits in my life with concentrating on watching, feeling, and breathing, while sitting for a length of time. It is surprising how unruly the mind can be. It might even be rather shocking when you first begin to focus your mind. At least it was for me.

I focus on my breath, since breath helps calm the mind. A technique I like is to pay special attention to the natural pause at the top and bottom of the breath. You can also intentionally extend this natural pause. When you come to the top of your inhalation, hold the breath in for a moment. Do not strain; only hold it in for a moment, while staying relaxed. Exhale, and hold the breath out for a moment. Continue to breathe this way, holding the breath in at the top of the inhalation, and out at the bottom of the exhalation. Focusing on these pauses helps to "pause" the mind.

Once the mind settles down, focus on your regular breath. Feel the sensations through the nostrils as you breathe normally; think of life force and energy coming into your body with every breath. As you focus your attention on your breath, feel any sensations in your body. Witness the thoughts in your mind. Whenever you notice you've been sucked into the thoughts, refocus your attention on the breath, sensations, and just Witness.

The breath is your anchor; so keep coming back to that. Witnessing your thoughts helps you more quickly realize you are no longer focused on your breath. It allows your thoughts to exist, but keeps you from becoming entangled in them. Focusing on breath and sensations helps you stay in the present moment.

As you focus on your breath you can also bring awareness to your third eye for extra stillness.

In summary: Close your eyes. Bring your attention to the third eye. Concentrate on your breath, especially the pause at the top and bottom of the breath. As thoughts bubble up, Witness them as though from a distance. Continue focusing on the breath and the third eye.

Sometimes the mind will be very stormy and cause strong sensations in the body. Witness the storm and sensations. Focus on your breath and the third eye as much as possible. Over time, the mind will become calmer, both in your sitting practice and in everyday life.

At some point, the thoughts will recede to the background and the breath will be in the foreground. It is not about emptying your mind of thoughts, as that would be impossible.

It is about using the breath to relax, and watching the thoughts come and go. As you watch your thoughts, detach from them. Try not to get caught up in the drama of your thoughts. They will dissipate simply by Witnessing them, so you do not need to try to stop them.

The mind is like a fast-moving train. The train does not suddenly come to a complete stop, it slows down over miles. Just slowing your mind down will give you much relief and insight. It will conserve your energy and allow you to relax. Maybe eventually you will empty your mind of thoughts and enter meditation. That isn't what you are practicing here. **You are practicing focusing and concentration.** If you happen to drop into a state of meditation, great! If not, great! There are tremendous benefits from being able to concentrate and slow down the mind.

MY EXPERIENCE WITH SITTING PRACTICE

When I first started my formal sitting practice, within five minutes I thought I would just die! My body was so restless and my mind so agitated. I was determined, though, that I was going to do this. Being in control of my mind could only be a tremendous benefit. I started out by setting a timer for fifteen minutes. Many teachers recommend thirty minutes. I could hardly bear fifteen. I figured, surely I can survive fifteen minutes a day of sitting with my restlessness.

I found a timer helpful because I didn't have to wonder if the fifteen minutes had passed. I practiced in the morning and had to be at work by a certain time, so it was important not to exceed the time I had allotted for my practice. I would put the timer under a towel to muffle it, so it would not sound so loud when it went off. In the beginning, those minutes felt like two hours! After a couple of months my restlessness subsided. I started adding five minutes every month, until I was sitting for thirty minutes a day.

As my restlessness abated, I went through a period of drowsiness. I became relaxed during sitting practice, and discovered that led to extreme sleepiness. Resisting the urge to fall asleep was as difficult as sitting with my earlier restlessness. I persevered, as I knew these were all phases every beginner goes through. It was just part of the process of training my mind to focus. After about three months, I noticed I was more often able to be relaxed and alert at the same time. I would still have periods of restlessness or drowsiness, but they became less frequent.

For quite some time my mind was so full of thoughts, plans, to-do lists, and other concerns, that I could hardly focus on my breath for more than a quarter of an inhale. I mostly watched my crowded mind, and refocused, refocused, refocused on my breath.

I might have given up had I not noticed beneficial changes in my life. Even though I felt like a concentration failure,

I must have been doing it right since I was becoming more calm and peaceful in my daily life. Things that used to bother me no longer affected me as much. I seemed to be less distracted when concentrating on work or other tasks.

As the years went by, my thoughts slowed down. I could concentrate on multiple breaths before my mind would get sucked into a thought. I would notice more quickly when I wasn't focused on my breath, and would resume my concentration. Now, although thoughts are still present, they are in the background. I more often have the thought of not thinking a thought. Not always, but many times, I look forward to my sitting practice, to the calm and peace I feel. Every day is different. Sometimes I still feel restless, yet never as much as when I first started.

When I resigned from my job and made the transition from North Carolina to Florida, I felt like my sitting practice regressed. I went through so much change and uncertainty that sitting with it was both a relief and a challenge. I had trouble concentrating during sitting practice, as my mind whirled over everything that needed doing, and everything that might or might not happen.

As I watched all of this, and focused as much as possible on my breath during my practice, it helped me stay present and clear all day while making decisions or concentrating on the many tasks I needed to accomplish. I once again noticed the effects of my practice in my daily life, even though I felt restless during the sitting practice itself.

I now trust that my sitting practice is working, whether I think it is or not. There will be plenty of times when you too will think, "I can't do this right, it isn't for me." I urge you to reflect on the results in your daily life, because the practice itself might or might not be what you think it should be. However, the benefits will show in your life. Sometimes my sitting practice is calm and peaceful; what I think of as "right." Other times my practice is restless. It has had a general progression of calming; it zigzags rather than going in a straight line.

As you practice connecting to your still center by withdrawing attention from the loud thoughts, the ups and downs of life become more of a dance than a tug of war. You quit wasting your energy from pushing away what you fear, and pulling toward you what you desire. You are more able to dance with reality, relaxing with the changing dance.

CONCENTRATION HELPED ME THROUGH A CRISIS

I was very grateful for my concentration practice while my dad was in the hospital with a complication from his lung surgery. I was taking care of my two-year-old niece for ten days, at my sister's house, while she and her husband traveled. After a couple of days, my parents decided to visit. It was two weeks after my dad had lung surgery, and he thought it would be more enjoyable to recover near his grandchild than at home. I'm sure it would have been, except he got an infection. By the second day, he had to go into the hospital.

I had just gotten used to being a temporary mommy. Now my dad was in ICU, and my mom was very worried and anxious. The doctors were not sure Dad would live. I was pushed to my edge with taking care of a toddler, worrying about Dad, and helping Mom.

The morning after Dad was admitted to the ICU, I took my niece to the park and pushed her in the swing. I was worried about Dad, and wondered if I was ever going to catch a break. It seemed like my life was one hardship after another. I was always taking care of others. That was what it felt like with my negative thoughts and worry. All of the sudden, I realized I was catching a break at that moment. The day was gorgeous, and my niece was smiling and laughing as I pushed her in the swing.

If I kept my attention on what was happening in the moment, nothing was wrong. In fact, everything was wonderful. I experienced that again, later in the day, when I was taking a walk, pushing my niece in the stroller. As I walked and worried about my dad, I began to concentrate on my feet making contact with the ground. I noticed the gentle breeze against my skin, and felt the warm sun seeping into my pores. There was a beautiful blooming sage bush up ahead, glowing in the sun. As I neared the bush, a flock of goldfinches flew off into a nearby tree. It was lovely to watch those birds flutter off at the same time. The sage smelled amazing as I walked by. It was such a beautiful moment. I was so glad to be able to experience it.

As long as I kept my attention focused in the present, my circumstances were tolerable. Plenty of times, they were even enjoyable. I could not have chosen what to focus my attention on if I had not practiced concentration over the years. The situation held too much emotional charge for me to have focused on the present, if I had not had some control over my mind.

The main way to gain control over the mind is to train it to concentrate on your chosen object, like paying attention to the breath during sitting practice. I was not able to stay focused on the present all the time. However, I could keep coming back to it, gaining immense relief by returning to the present moment.

By concentrating on the present, instead of my worried thoughts, I was able to be with my dad in a peaceful, relaxed manner during the hospital visits. I could also help my mom remain calm. I had more energy to be helpful, because I wasn't wasting it on anxiety. I could choose where to place my focus: the now, or the uncertain future with, or without, my dad. Luckily, Dad's condition improved. After a couple weeks, he was released from the hospital.

The ability to choose what you concentrate on, and to sustain that concentration, allows you to direct your life and experience peace. This is why practicing concentration is never a wasted effort. Often, I would feel like I couldn't concentrate in sitting practice because I could only focus on a couple of breaths at a time. Sometimes not even that much.

With even a small amount of concentration, I have been able to find the peace of the present moment in times of crisis. With a little more concentration, I have often experienced complete enjoyment of the present moment during stress-free times. The formal practice of concentrating, affects your daily life in a positive way. Even if you think your sitting practice is not going well, it is still having a positive effect in your daily life.

MAKING TIME FOR FORMAL PRACTICE

Although there are so many ways to practice these techniques informally throughout the day, it is important to set aside a little time each day to practice stillness and silence. It is in this space of quiet that we tap into our deep inner wisdom of higher consciousness. This is a powerful force of love and wisdom. It changes your life, and gives you the peace and contentment you seek. Although this force is everywhere, you can only access it from within. It is so powerful that even practicing only fifteen minutes a day will have an effect.

I know you are thinking, "OMG! How am I going to add one more thing to my life?" That is why I recommend starting with fifteen minutes. I notice many people feel like a hamster, running round and round on that wheel in the cage. They do not like how crazy and tiring their life has become. However, they do not know what to do about it, so they just keep running until one day they collapse. They become ill, or their world comes crashing down on their head. So go within, to tap into wisdom for fifteen minutes a day, before your world comes to a crisis.

When you make a sincere, consistent effort to create space, you let the universe know that you mean it. The universe will respond by giving you more space. It is similar to when someone asks you for help. If you notice they are doing nothing to help themselves, you are not too motivated to help them. If they are really trying to make a change, using their own effort, you feel good about helping them.

The energy of the universe responds in the same way. If you do nothing except complain about your life, the universe does not take your desire for peace seriously. You have to first show that you are serious about the change you want.

In our busy schedules, fifteen minutes is a good place to begin. Perhaps you can even manage fifteen minutes twice a day. As you tap into the Witness, your actions will become more efficient, which will free up more time to practice.

Start with the intention to make time for practice. Then, Witness yourself throughout the day. Do this for a week or two. You will discover how to make the time for practice. Notice where you waste time, or an activity you can forgo. Since life is so busy, you will likely need to eliminate something for fifteen minutes once a day to add the time for practice. It will be well worth it!

Practice is a sure way to integrate these techniques and gain insight about what changes to make and how to make them. Practice accesses the creative source within, giving you access to real solutions. Without practice, everything you read or listen to is just theory. The only effect that will have is entertainment.

Try some of these suggestions for introducing a practice within a busy schedule:

- Sit in a parked car for ten minutes, focusing on your breath, before heading into work or the house. (When you slow down your breath, you slow down your mind.)

- Spend an extra several minutes when you go to the bathroom. Take a stretching and breathing break.

- When you take a shower, stay a little longer. Feel the water on your skin as you take deep breaths.

- Go to bed ten minutes early, and do full belly to chest breaths or a sitting meditation.

As you introduce these meditation breaks, it will help to open up the space to practice longer, building up to thirty minutes a day.

As you incorporate a daily practice into your schedule, you will see the benefits, which will motivate you to continue. At some point, the practice builds its own momentum. For example, you have brushed your teeth for so long you no longer have to debate if you will brush your teeth before bed or not. It has built up momentum, and you just do it. The same will occur with your sitting practice.

INFORMAL FOCUSING PRACTICE

Another way to practice concentration is to choose a daily activity and focus your attention on it fully. Choose something simple like brushing your teeth, or walking to your car. Every time you realize you have lost focus on brushing your teeth, bring your attention back to the activity. Feel the sensations of the brush on your teeth. Witness yourself doing the activity. Your mind will wander every split second at first; simply bring it back. If you do this on a daily basis, choosing just one activity, your concentration will improve immensely.

This is a way to practice without having to make extra time in your schedule. You do your chosen activity anyway, so now you are just practicing your concentration while doing it. I like to make it into a game. When I take a walk, I say to myself, "Can I concentrate on sensations and breath from here to that tree?" I'll see how far I get before my mind wanders. In the beginning, I would say, "Can I focus for two steps?" I used to have a two-story house. I would see how far up or down the stairs I could get before losing my focus. As your powers of concentration improve, you will notice yourself become more efficient, wasting less time and energy.

FINDING HOME THROUGH PRACTICE

In January of 2010, my husband and I made the decision to separate, sell our house, and leave North Carolina. Once we made this decision, I no longer had a home. As I fixed up the house, transforming it into the vision we had, it was necessary to stay detached, or else it would be too difficult to leave. I worked hard to make our house into a beautiful home for its future owner.

During this time, I stayed consistent with my yoga practice, on and off my mat. With detachment, I Witnessed my feelings and thoughts as I worked on the house, as my husband packed up to leave, and as I wondered how long I would be there by myself. I did a lot of deep, slow breathing to stay present with all of this.

My yoga mat became a welcome relief for my body and mind as the gentle stretches, breath work, and meditation helped dissolve the tension of all the labor and uncertainty. No matter how tired or busy I was, I still did my formal practice on the mat. It provided the only structure in my life in the midst of so much change. I came to realize I could count on my practice, which would be there for me every time I rolled out my mat. At some point, I realized my practice had become the ground under my feet, and it led me to my true Home inside myself.

I could call no physical place home, yet oddly, I was at Home. Now, no matter where I am, or whom I'm with, I am at Home. After the house sold, I moved in with a family friend for several months, before moving in with my parents. Connection to my Home within gave me the security and stability I needed during all the moving around.

For a practice to bring you Home, it must be consistent. This means that you practice when you do not want to practice, when you are sick, when you are well, when you are tired, happy, or feeling any other emotion. If you have a house you call home, you go there when you are sick or well, tired or happy. No matter how you feel, you go home. The same is true with your practice. No matter how you feel, your practice will bring you to your Home within, if you practice.

PRACTICE SHOWS YOU HOW UNCOMMITTED YOU ARE

You say you want less stress and more peace in your life. You want to experience the joy of life, not just get through each day. However, you don't want to spend even fifteen minutes a day practicing to achieve that peace.

The good news is that the same practice that shows you how uncommitted you are, also strengthens your commitment over time. As you stick with the practice, it begins to stick with you. As you take care of your practice, it will take care of you. You will begin experiencing the peace and joy you are committed to live.

Pema Chodron, a well-known Buddhist nun and teacher, says that monastic life is extremely challenging because there are no exits. You cannot escape from yourself or your issues. You are forced to face your pain, sadness, anger, or whatever else comes up. This is why some solitude in daily practice is important. Since you are not in a monastery, closing off the exits will have to come from discipline, and through your commitment to lead a more peaceful and joyful life.

I find practicing in worldly life to be extremely challenging because there are so many exits. All of your issues are with you everywhere you go, affecting you in subconscious ways. They remain with you longer, because you can easily avoid dealing with them. It is a challenge to practice when the world encourages you to avoid and forget.

The world also is a mirror, reflecting your unresolved issues in the form of your reactions. Your reactions to people, places, and situations, reveal what is unresolved within you.

The things that cause you to react are a powerful opportunity to practice these techniques, to resolve your issues and your past.

The world will also show you your progress, as what used to cause you to react, no longer does. You find you experience more peace in situations that used to cause stress. The world is a wonderful, direct teacher, showing you how far you have come, as well as how far you need to go.

KAYAKING THE RIVER OF LIFE

Practicing yoga in the midst of life reminds me of kayaking down a river. When you paddle downriver, you use your skills to both go with the flow of current and to navigate where you want to within the river. If you run into trouble and capsize, you roll up, and continue to paddle. As you hone your skills on the river, you learn to read the water, discovering how to maneuver. It is a combination of going with the flow and setting your own direction.

If you do not go with the river, relying only on yourself, you expend a lot of energy fighting the current. You easily become exhausted. The fun the river can hold turns into a battle you hope to win, but never do. Conversely, if you just bob along with the current, doing nothing, the river becomes a fearful obstacle course you hope to get through alive. It takes the flow of the river, plus your skill in action, to relax and have fun. You are being directed, and you are directing.

If you have been paddling for a while and need to rest, the river will provide that for you, if you take the opportunity. Even in the turbulent rapids, there are small eddies where you can park your boat for a moment, rest, and decide your next move. When you need more rest, you paddle over to the bank and get out for a while, maybe have some lunch. The more skilled you are, the more rest and play you can enjoy, and the more opportunities you can discover and use.

When you do nothing, or do everything, you miss the joy in the River of Life. When you resist the flow, or bob along with no paddling skills, you put yourself in danger. Your life is filled with suffering. Go down the River of Life with a combination of skillful action from practice, setting your direction, and flowing with the current. The River of Life can be great fun, providing enjoyment, rest, and calm, when you are skillful enough to go with the flow. The same river can be a fun playground, or your worst nightmare. It all depends on how you work with it, and your level of skill.

The main difference between paddling the River of Life, and paddling on water, is that the life skills transfer to everything you do, while the water skills are good only while you are on the water. When you finish paddling down the water rapids, there is no more skill in action. If you are skilled with the yoga strokes of Witnessing, feeling, and breathing, you are skilled with everything in your life.

Chapter
6

Spiritual Practice
with Life

INTEGRATION

Integration means to bring parts together to create a whole, to unify. For a long time I felt like my life was compartmentalized. I had work life, home life, leisure life, and yoga-teaching life. All four were major areas that seemed separate from each other. Trying to juggle them tired me out. I had four selves to keep up with!

As I learned and practiced the integrative techniques of Witnessing, breathing, and feeling sensations, I noticed, over time, that these areas became less compartmentalized. I practiced yoga at work with the everyday tasks, stress, and drama, which made me more efficient and creative. I practiced the core yoga techniques with teaching, with washing dishes, answering the phone, problem solving, riding my bike, and going on hikes. I would practice while relaxing and having fun with my friends and family. The core practice permeated all areas of my life. I no longer felt the different parts of my life were separate from each other.

Everything I did was yoga practice, just different types of "poses." Sometimes the pose was answering the phone, sometimes it was getting a performance review at work, or going on a hike, or playing tennis, or collecting unemployment. Everything became an opportunity to practice. Eventually this felt less like a practice and more like how I lived.

SPIRITUALITY

We often think of being spiritual as a wonderful, otherworldly experience, and it certainly can be. However, the practice to become more spiritual often involves discipline, working with the "down and dirty" of daily life. Jack Kornfield phrases it well in the title of his book *After the Ecstasy, the Laundry.* I also like Eckhart Tolle's book, *The Power of Now.* Sometimes "now" can be singing, chanting, dancing, and being blissed out. Most of the time, "now" is cleaning the house, paying the bills, making and returning phone calls, attending meetings, studying for tests, mowing the lawn... you get the picture.

As you fold the laundry, be present with the activity. Feel the texture of the clothes in your hands, smell the aroma left from the detergent, feel your muscles flex as you pick up the stack of folded shorts and place them in the drawer. Your mind will lose its resistance to the chore if you are present, focused on the sensations of the activity. This will help you move from doing to being. When you are being, you are in spirit, connected to life. You simply enjoy whatever is before you, because you are present with it. Enjoy the music, singing, and dancing, but through practice, also learn to enjoy washing dishes and vacuuming.

As you practice paying attention and being present with all of your daily duties you become more spiritual, which means, being more patient, kind, loving, and compassionate. You increase your capacity to be at peace with different people and situations. Spirituality is as simple as being relaxed and present with whatever comes your way. This is not easy, though. It requires constant practice.

The Bhagavad Gita, a Hindu scripture, describes the Lord as "If a thousand suns were to rise in the heavens at the same time, the blaze of their light would resemble the splendor of that supreme spirit." (11:12) We are unable to look at our one sun for long without going blind, let alone "a thousand suns."

I had a tiny taste of this divine energy when I was in high school. I didn't believe in God, yet I was searching, and open to the possibility. For several months I would silently chant "God, grant me thy peace" every night while falling asleep. After about three months, I had the most amazing peace and bliss fill me. It was so intense it scared me. I felt I would die of bliss if it continued.

This is why the spiritual journey to know God is paved in discipline and purification. "For the Lord disciplines the one he loves, and chastises every son whom he receives." (Holy Bible, *English Standard Version*, Heb. 12:6)

I like the analogy of bathing a dirty child. The child just wants to splash around and play in the water. She does not like it when you get the washcloth out and scrub a bit to clean off the dirt. Once you are finished, and the child is clean, you take her out of the tub to dry her off. You do not keep washing her once she is clean.

If you have a wound, you need to clean out the dirt so it can heal. It can be painful while you clean it. You do it anyway so you can heal. Life is just like bathing the child or cleaning a wound. It doesn't necessarily give you what you want. It will give you what you need to become clean and luminous, more loving, and more in the image of your true self.

CODES OF CONDUCT

Religions and societies all have codes of conduct. So does the eight-limbed system of yoga. This is not to punish you, rather its purpose is to help you on your spiritual journey. Our ego-mind, emotional attachments, and aversions, cover up our intuition and wisdom. By checking your "intuition" against the code of conduct, you can determine if your actions are coming from ego or wisdom. It is a check and balance system for "right" living.

The more you practice in reference to the code of conduct, the more you can rely on your intuition and live from wisdom. The more you practice, the more you access your higher self, and the more you will want to follow the codes of conduct. Going against them will not even be attractive to you.

In yoga, these codes are called *yamas* and *niyamas*. The *yamas* are guidelines for how to interact with people and situations. The *niyamas* are observances that deal with your inner world. I have listed them below:

Yamas

- Non-violence in thought, word, and deed
- Truthfulness or honesty
- Non-stealing
- Moderation
- Non-possessiveness or non-greed

Niyamas

- Purity of body, mind, and heart
- Contentment
- Self-discipline
- Self-study with non-judgment
- Surrender to God

Perhaps you dislike someone. You think "Yay! I can be honest and tell them how I really feel." The first *yama* is non-violence. All the others are aspects of non-violence. If being honest needlessly hurts someone, or causes even mild violence, restrain from speaking your mind.

As you continue to check your intuition, thoughts, and actions, with the *yamas* and *niyamas*, you will find the still small voice of spirit becomes stronger. You will be able to access wisdom, and find it is naturally in accordance with the codes of conduct. As you identify less with your ego, you will automatically be in tune with the *yamas* and *niyamas*.

THE SPIRITUAL HEART

According to research at the Institute of HeartMath, the heart is the body's most powerful electromagnetic transmitter. It is fifty times stronger than the brain's electromagnetic field, and detectable from eight to twelve feet away. Research also suggests that the heart is a direct link to subtle energy that contains information on objects and events in their energetic form, before physical manifestation. In other words, a direct knowing or intuition.

We all have access to this direct knowing from the heart. Many of you have likely experienced it. Even predictions of the future are not uncommon. However, our mind will usually discount the information, because it doesn't arrive in a logical way. After ignoring it long enough, we shut ourselves off from this energetic knowledge from the heart.

Instead of a clear heart connected to universal energy and wisdom, we live with an emotional heart, subject to our ego-mind's fears, insecurities, and choices. The emotional heart is reactive and dramatic, a slave to our attachments, aversions, past habits, and patterns. Acting from attachments and aversions strengthen the emotional heart, which is fed by the ego. Instead of receiving information from wisdom, we receive information based in our fears and insecurities, and call it intuition.

The clear heart that accesses wisdom is unconditional and has no need to make choices. It is free of attachment and aversion, and knows what is best for your true self. It is not uncommon to receive information your ego-mind doesn't like, but that you *know* is in your best interest. The clear heart is a guiding light urging you forward. It has tremendous strength and resilience, allowing you to weather whatever lessons life has in store for you. As you go through hard times, embracing life totally, you move ever closer to the peace, joy, and freedom, of the unemotional heart.

The yoga practice of Witnessing, feeling, and breathing, helps you tap into this heart wisdom and strength, helps the mind relax and go with the heart, that though illogical, knows directly. You become freer to relax with the flow of life, reducing suffering, thus experiencing more joy. Without a practice, your attachments and aversions will confuse you. You will be unable to access the clarity of heart wisdom.

You can easily mistake your attachment as the "right" thing to do. Consistent practice is essential in accessing the unconditional love of the unemotional heart.

As you use your practice to relax with what is, as it is, you break through your reactive patterns, and begin to access the spiritual heart more often. Even if you've made a "bad" decision from your emotional heart, as you relax with your situation and accept it, you will tap into wisdom. Eventually you gain clarity about how to adjust the situation if it doesn't resolve on its own. Your "bad" decision becomes a good one that you've used to clear your emotional heart.

LIVING FROM THE FEELING CENTER AND HEART

When I married my husband, loved ones considered that a "bad" decision. In addition to being unemployed, he had some health problems. Although it appeared to others that I made a mistake, it felt right in my heart, so I went with it. It turned out to be a marriage that was the right choice for my highest good, and it helped me access my spiritual heart.

I had a kind, compassionate husband who, over seven years, taught me many lessons in patience, compassion, commitment, and inner strength. It was a marriage that, due to circumstances, encouraged me to rely on my yoga practice to relax through the challenges, and brought me closer to God. My marriage was not easy, yet it was always right.

Because the decision was made from my heart, I had the strength to stay committed while learning the life lessons it offered. Plenty of times, my mind wanted out, but because it felt right, I could stay.

Eventually circumstances shifted. We both knew life was putting us on different paths. Divorce was inevitable. The marriage had served its purpose, and now it was time for it to dissolve. Everyone was mystified at how easily we were able to part ways. Since the decision came from life, it was right. We both knew to follow the signs life was presenting. That is not to say there wasn't sadness. But I could relax with it, and let the sadness come and go. I could allow the sadness to move through me.

I needed the lessons I learned from my marriage. They strengthened my practice, giving me the confidence to follow my heart and know it is right. I used my practice to grow spiritually, and to gain trust in life.

As I use my practice to relax and accept life on its terms, I clear my emotional heart, so I may access the wisdom of my spiritual heart. I know more what to do, and what not to do, as opportunities show up, whether it is an idea to try, or an offer to accept. I never know what heart wisdom will attract to my life. All kinds of situations, people, and circumstances, appear when the time is right. The mind, although important, limits me from living to my full potential. The mind is only comfortable with the known; the spiritual dimension is unknown. Using heart wisdom, life goes from being an obstacle course, to being an adventure.

When situations or circumstances are challenging, because the decisions come from my heart and feelings, I have the commitment and steadfastness to stay the course. It may appear to others that I make decisions in haste. This is because the heart knows immediately. I bypass the lengthy process of pros and cons, analysis and doubt. One certainly needs the mental process to execute plans and carry out decisions, but the heart is the best place to make the initial decision if what you want out of life is for your highest good.

Chapter

7

Become What You Want to Be

PRACTICING WITH OPPOSITES

I would like to be loving, kind, and patient. To acquire these qualities I have to practice them. To practice patience, I have to experience impatience, which is usually not a problem! You cannot know light if you have no experience of dark. You cannot understand tall if there is no short. As long as you do not choose one over the other, opposites coexist in harmony.

In fact, you need the negative qualities to help you move toward the positive ones. You cannot be patient or kind if there is no reason to do so. If I get in the checkout line behind someone who is sorting through her coupons, paying with a personal check, and taking forever, I get an opportunity to practice patience. I can Witness the feelings of frustration, and observe the negative comments in my mind. I Witness, and feel, my impatience. I deepen my breath. As I relax and feel the sensations, I realize waiting is okay. I become patient while I wait.

I work with kindness in the same way. When someone is unkind, she shows me the unkindness within myself. This gives me an opportunity to practice. I see the unkindness in me when I notice my resistance to being nice to someone who is not nice. I notice I would like to tell them off. If I react in an unkind way, I notice my reaction and experience it. I practice accepting and relaxing with the unkindness in me. That alone allows me to transform my unkindness into kindness.

To be kind in the face of kindness is not that difficult; it doesn't take much to do that. It is when you can be kind in the face of the unkind that you are truly kind.

MY WAITING PRACTICE

I used to get impatient and hated waiting in lines, at doctor offices, or at traffic lights. Like most people, my days were extremely busy, packed with a long list of things to do. I found waiting very frustrating because I had all this stuff to do. I had places to be!

At some point, it occurred to me that I wasn't hurrying anything along by being upset about it. In fact, I wasted a lot of energy in being frustrated, which made me more tired. I decided to change my attitude, and think of waiting as an opportunity to rest. I was often so busy rushing around and multi-tasking, I could use a rest break. Coming up to a traffic light, I feel my body tense up. I could Witness my thought of "Oh come on! Turn green!" As I watched my thoughts of "hurry up," and felt the tension in my body, I would remind myself to relax. I would unclench my grip on the steering wheel, take some deep breaths, and begin to relax. Soon I felt at ease.

I would do this whenever I found myself in a waiting situation, and discovered I felt less drained at the end of the day. I would not have been able to change my attitude if I hadn't Witnessed my habit of frustration, and relaxed with the feeling of my tense muscles. Now, I usually don't mind waiting. I even feel better for it.

I even found ways to incorporate waiting "rest breaks" at work, which most of you know is no easy task. The work place is filled with tension and rushing. The deadline for all projects is yesterday. I used to design fabric for home furnishings, working my way up to senior designer. Like most people in the work force, I felt pulled in a million directions at once.

It was a challenge to be creative and design beautiful fabric when I didn't have a moment to think! Since I was Witnessing my thoughts, I was able to create some detachment to see clearly what could be done with this frantic situation. My practice allowed me to carve out moments of space for myself, and notice where I wasted my energy.

Whenever my phone rang, I noticed my instinct to grab it immediately; yet I would refrain, taking one or two deep breaths before I answered it. Soon my ringing phone became a reminder to breathe and relax. I found this also made me more helpful to the person on the other end.

When I took a bathroom break, I would breathe, and feel my feet make contact with the floor while I walked to the bathroom. I did not talk on the cell phone while on the toilet! I used the time to relax and relieve my bladder.

By Witnessing my thoughts and actions, I realized that multi-tasking only gave me the illusion of achieving more. In reality, it drained me and reduced my concentration. Although I had an urgent "to-do" pile on my desk, as much as possible, I focused on only one task at a time. If I was in the middle of a task when something more urgent arose, I made a note of where I left off, and began the new, more urgent task. I would forget about the previous task, focusing all my attention on the new one.

If my phone rang in the middle of something I couldn't break concentration with, I would let it go to voicemail. As soon as I was at a stopping point, I returned the call. This way everything got my full attention, one thing at a time. I could reprioritize throughout the day as needed. I found I accomplished much more, and my work was top quality. After a while, my coworkers even told me to slow down because I was making them look bad! Yet I rarely hurried. I was focused, in the moment, and relaxed, allowing me the energy to get a tremendous amount of work accomplished. Since I got so much done this way, I rarely had to stay late.

I made a point to take a ten-minute walk around the building in the afternoon, just to breathe and feel the sensations of walking. If you use your walk to complain to a co-worker, you won't get any relaxation benefit. I also walked across the hall a couple times a day, just to look out the window while taking several breaths. Then I walked back to my desk and continued to work.

Practicing this way, taking present moment mini-breaks, conserved my energy, making me very efficient in a challenging environment. My co-workers and boss even started practicing some of these techniques as they saw how relaxed and productive I was.

My relaxed attitude helped those around me relax, too. When someone feels stressed, they look and act stressed. If you are around those people, their attitude and actions will affect you, causing you stress. This is a vicious, escalating cycle.

If you are around someone who is happy, smiling, and nice to you, soon you feel happy. When I was relaxed at work, my co-workers and boss could relax more. There were times my boss was so stressed she would take it out on the rest of us. I felt strong sensations of discomfort in my body during those moments, but was able to just feel them and watch my thoughts without getting caught up in the drama. I would take deep breaths. Some of the discomfort and heat would subside.

As I did not react to my boss, her anger and stress had nothing to push against, and I could feel her begin to calm down. As I would listen to her and breathe without reacting, she would begin to relax. When I did need to respond, I chose my words carefully, speaking them calmly. As I talked, she would grow calmer. Soon the episode would pass, and we could find a creative solution to the problem.

Sometimes my boss would be upset about something she told me to do, which she would later forget she told me. Sometimes I even had an email or proof of her instructions. I would not remind her though, as it was not important that I be right. It was more important that we find a good resolution to the problem.

I would watch my ego have a hard time with this, as I took the blame for something I was told to do. As I watched my desire to prove I was right, yet did nothing about it, my ego would give up. I returned to peace and calm. So did my boss. Taking the blame never affected my performance reviews. The situation was soon forgotten. What she remembered was the resolution, my efficiency, and my calm attitude.

You cannot change other people, but you can change yourself. When you change, you act and respond differently, which affects others. Many times you will notice people and situations change around you because of the way you respond to them. When you react angrily to a situation, you escalate the situation, and it usually turns out badly. If you respond calmly, the situation usually diffuses itself, creating a more pleasant outcome. **You have not changed anyone except yourself, yet that changes everything.**

LISTENING TO OTHERS

Another way I practice being loving and patient is by listening to others. If you pay attention, you will notice many times when someone talks you are half-way listening. Mostly, you are thinking about what you want to say as soon as she finishes. Or you are not listening at all. Instead, you are thinking of all the stuff you need to do. On a subconscious level, people sense when you are not paying attention. They talk even more, or speak louder. I'm sure you have experienced not being heard. It is a lonely, frustrating feeling, that happens often, and we just get used to it.

The next time you are in a conversation with someone, really listen. Watch yourself listening. You will notice how the mind keeps the internal dialog constantly running during the conversation. As you realize this, keep returning your focus to what the other person is saying. Let your mental chatter recede to the background as you bring your friend's voice to the foreground. The conversation you are having becomes your point of focus for being present. Your friend or partner will feel you listening, and love you more for it.

At one point, I joined a group of people who practice mindful listening and sharing. Often this was with a group of eight to twenty people. Someone would acknowledge that they had something to say. Everyone would take a couple of deep breaths before that person would say what was on their mind or heart. While they talked, the rest of us would practice listening; no one would cut them off or try to talk over them.

Once the person finished, they acknowledged to the group that they were done. We would all take a couple of deep breaths again, before someone else could acknowledge they had something to say. This way the person who had been speaking knew they had been heard. The group did not offer any advice unless the person specifically requested it.

After a couple of months, I realized how richly rewarding this practice was. The group was like a safe, empty container into which I could put whatever I wanted. No one was going to try to "fix" what I put in this container. My own inner wisdom was allowed to surface in this safe, compassionate group of listeners. If anything I shared needed a solution, the answer would arise from the empty container.

Many times, the best solution to problems is to speak them aloud, and know someone hears. It is also therapeutic to be the listener, to get out of your head while you truly listen to someone, connecting to their heart. Listen to their pain. Listen to their joy. Connecting, being an empty container for someone else, will bring you both closer. It is very therapeutic to connect to other humans on a deep inner level. Try this with your young children, your teens, your partner, and friends. You can tell your family or friends that you want to experiment with this, and openly practice together. Or you can practice listening, without telling them. Either way, they will feel your listening.

POSITIVE QUALITIES

Whatever you place your attention on, you feed with energy. If you focus on the negative, people and situations will become more troublesome. Your world will be full of conflict.

Try focusing on all the good qualities in the people you know. This will change your attitude about them, as well as your actions toward them. As you nurture their good qualities, they will sense that, and act more lovingly. You will be able to feel more accepting of those around you. Their negative qualities won't bother you so much. This also gives them the space to be more accepting of you, because they feel more loved and secure.

There are people I consider good friends who have major shortcomings. They also have very good qualities. I recognize both, but focus on the good. Some people I know I can count on. Some, I know I can't. When you just accept people as they are, focusing on their good qualities, you can be friends with many people. Their negative qualities diminish, because you are not feeding those with your energy. They recede to the background, and the good qualities come to the foreground.

As you see the good qualities in others, it will help them see the good qualities in themselves. They will feel loved, and that will help them love themselves. With love, their negative habits will naturally diminish over time.

Try this as an experiment. Choose a person you like, in whom you find some annoying traits. Focus on what you like about that person. When you find yourself mentally or verbally complaining about him, stop, and refocus on what you like. See how the relationship begins to change. Try the same technique with a place, or situation. Perhaps you will want to try this where you work. Focus on what is going well. When you find yourself paying attention to the negative, redirect your thoughts to what is positive.

Chapter 8

Supportive Practices

WHEN LIFE IS TOO CHALLENGING

Sometimes life has given me challenges that were way beyond my edge and I needed extra help in addition to Witnessing, breathing, and feeling. The following are some practices I have found supportive to my main practice when life gets tough.

INSPIRATIONAL READING

I like inspirational reading during times of struggle. Inspirational listening would work fine too, in case you prefer podcasts or other media. I happen to be spiritual in nature, so I gravitate to a variety of devotional, God-related reading. Not everyone feels this way, so anything that you find inspiring or uplifting will be helpful. Perhaps you prefer poetry about nature, or maybe science is more your thing. I especially turn to inspirational reading during times of uncertainty and instability. I first practiced this in earnest while working at one of my first jobs in the textile industry.

Six months after hiring me, the company started the first of many years of regular lay-offs and reorganizations. Due to the Free Trade Agreement with China, the entire American textile industry downsized.

There was a tremendous amount of uncertainty as my co-workers were let go over the years. I worried I would be next. The mind tends to go to the worst-case scenario, especially when your future is uncertain. Since my job paid the mortgage and all of the bills, what would I do if I lost my paycheck? I'd be homeless, living under a bridge! I'd be starving in the park!

My negative worst-case thoughts created much anxiety. I would Witness the negativity and worry to remove the drama. I would feel the knot in the pit of my stomach as my co-workers received summons to the conference room, where they were dismissed from employment. I would feel my heart race as I wondered if I would be next. I kept my breath long and deep, gave space to the worry and fear, allowing them to exist, as I simply Witnessed everything. The sensations would ebb and flow; sometimes they were strong, sometimes weak. Even with all of my yoga techniques, it didn't seem to be quite enough. Although my practice reduced the anxiety, fear still lurked in the background.

Along with the rest of my practice, inspirational reading helped me surrender and trust that all was well. I have a book of various sacred world scripture from all kinds of traditions—religious and non-religious. The common theme is that some power greater than me is taking care of things, even if I do not intellectually understand it.

I found it very powerful that so many different sources said the same thing in different ways. For me, this kind of reading did the trick. For you it might be other types. As I perused the passages, I would focus my attention on the words, reading slowly. I would feel the calm sensations begin to enter my heart, and feel my chest relax. This way, I was fully present with what I read. I could let it really sink in.

If you just skim the pages while you keep worrying, and do not concentrate on the words or message, it will not have much effect. I felt immediate relief with this practice. After a while, I felt much calmer all the time; even at work, during layoff days. There were still periods of turmoil, but I was able to feel the underlying peace, even in the face of tremendous uncertainty.

I worked at my job six years before they finally closed the doors, making it necessary for me to collect unemployment. When I was one of the names called to the conference room, given papers to sign, told to pack my personal belongings, and walked out the door, it was okay. Even though I did not know what was going to happen next, I was relaxed, and could feel an underlying peace. I somehow knew I would be just fine.

NATURE

Nature is a wonderful place for spiritual practice. I find it very soothing, a tremendous relief, to immerse myself in the outdoors when life throws the tough stuff at me. Often, we miss these benefits, because we take our worries with us when we hike in the mountains or walk on the beach. In order to enjoy nature, and experience her soothing effect, you need to be present.

Feel the sensations of the breeze against your skin, and the fragrance of the air. Are you in a forest, or on a beach? The air in both places feels and smells different. What do you feel beneath your feet when you walk, or beneath your body when you sit or lie down? What sounds do you hear? If you pick a tomato in your garden, how does it feel in your hand?

Pay close attention to sight, sound, and touch while you immerse yourself in nature. Notice how beautiful that little bird is that just alighted on your feeder. Pay attention to the aromas around you. Are they earthy or salty? Perhaps there is a flower blooming nearby with a delicious fragrance. How beautifully delicate it looks! Did you really see it? There is nothing to worry about when you are present with harvesting vegetables, planting seeds, petting your cat or dog, walking on the beach, or observing the birds. Nature is a soothing balm that uplifts me whether I'm happy, angry, sad, or neutral.

HUSBAND'S ILLNESS

Being present in nature helped get me through the years of my husband's illness. We had been married about two years when he started having various health problems. They were vague and mysterious, which made them difficult to diagnose. He would tire easily, had digestive problems, and a low tolerance to stress. Eventually he came down with a blistery, itchy, skin rash that would not go away. After nine months with this horrible condition, he finally received a diagnosis of celiac disease, an autoimmune disorder. Once we learned how to eliminate gluten from his diet, the rash disappeared, and the other symptoms began to diminish.

His symptoms continued to improve for a while, but suddenly his health completely crashed. He had very little energy to do anything. We would try to take a walk in the neighborhood. Within five minutes, he would have to sit on the curb while I went to get the car to pick him up. He would manage to shuffle into the house, plop on the couch, and sleep for several hours. It was as if someone flipped an energy switch, and suddenly, he stopped in his tracks.

This went on for several months before we were finally able to get a diagnosis of adrenal fatigue syndrome. This is a stress-related disorder, likely caused by the celiac disease, my layoffs, and our frequent moves. Once he got on supplements and hormones, his health very slowly improved over the years.

This period of illness was quite a challenge for me. I loved him. At the same time, I resented having no financial or domestic help. I had no partner for activities, no one to share hikes, bike rides, or walks. He needed my care, but I was so drained I couldn't always give it. I sometimes felt he was more like a son to me than a husband. I was worried about him, and I was worried about me. I could see no end in sight. I felt like this would be my marriage and life forever.

I needed to dig deep into my practice so I could soften my resistance to the situation in order to have the energy to help him. In addition to my usual practice of Witnessing, feeling, and breathing, I sought the comfort of the plants, animals, and outdoors.

Sometimes I would lie on the grass in the backyard, look up at the trees, and practice being present, so I could feel connected to the earth. I noticed the support of Mother Earth beneath my body, and would relax and release into her. I imagined an umbilical cord from my navel to the center of the earth, and felt the nurturing, grounding presence of Mother. Being present with nature gave me the strength to support my husband, and myself.

Tending to the vegetables and herbs in my backyard garden gave me great comfort. I would touch and smell the plants, notice the bugs, and listen to the birds. When my mind turned to thoughts of worry, I would refocus on the life around me. By paying close attention to nature, I could feel her energy seep into my tired body, soothing my heart. She would compassionately listen to me cry without comment, holding me in her green embrace. By practicing to relax, I was able to allow nature to be my Mother, and to receive her comfort. She did not judge me, or my husband. She was just a loving presence giving me the strength and energy to care for, and love, my husband.

LIFE SUPPORT

Another practice I often use, is remembering all the ways life supports me. This has been especially helpful when I feel scared or unsupported. Noticing this also gives me the courage to follow my heart as life leads me into unknown territory. Your heart is your inner guide that will bring you toward your soul.

I've always believed following your heart is your true path. The mind's job is to implement the plan the heart wants. Although this can be most rewarding, it can also be very difficult in the beginning, especially if it goes against the collective thoughts of the people around you. Following your heart requires trust, but our society lives by reason.

The heart path feels risky, unlike the mind's path, which plans for safety. When safety turns into stagnation, it is time to move on and follow the heart. When I notice or remember the support I receive from life, it gives me the strength to go with my heart, replacing those thoughts of doubt and fear with thoughts of comfort.

Often, support comes in a thousand small, and even big, ways we tend to overlook. When I moved out of North Carolina, I was by myself, and had to get rid of my furniture. As I wondered how to go about this, I received a call from my realtor who told me the couple buying my house wanted to purchase a lot of the furniture. After I sold most to that couple, a co-worker offered to come over with her husband, and a pickup truck, to take the remaining furniture to a consignment shop.

My 1997 Honda needed some expensive repairs. I didn't know how I would come up with the money to repair my car or buy a newer one. Not long after this, my parents bought a new car, and gave me their older model, which was in better condition than my Honda.

A couple of years after I moved back to Florida, I wanted to rent a small house in a specific location. Everyone told me there would be nothing available within my budget. I called a realtor anyway. Sure enough, there was a tiny efficiency house, within my budget, located in my preferred area. When I looked at the house it was perfect!

I can think of so many ways, both small and large, where people, places, and events, have worked out for me. Sometimes it is only with hindsight that I realize this. In the end, I know I am completely supported by life.

Be aware of the circumstances you feed with your energy. If you take notice of the times life supports you, that support will grow and be available more often. Even if you think you lack support, I'm sure you can find unacknowledged blessings in your life. Did you eat today? Do you have a bed to sleep on, or a roof over your head? Even if you are worried about tomorrow, do you have a roof over your head now?

Any support you have now will multiply as you focus your attention and look for the ways life supports you. This will also help you trust life and people. Usually, we focus on the negative, and then wonder why our life is so hard and we are so unhappy. Focus on positive thoughts. Your life will become more enjoyable.

INTENTIONS

Intentions are like guiding lights, keeping you on a set direction. They are not goal- or result-oriented; rather they help you move in a clear direction. The mind has limits. When you have goals, you confine yourself to those limitations. Goals do have a purpose, and there are times you do need to limit yourself to a specific goal.

An intention serves a different purpose. With an intention, you are opening yourself to the field of pure potential, where anything is possible. It sets a direction, so you can keep from getting lost. You do not arrive at your intention, because its purpose is to keep you moving. Therefore, unlimited possibilities are available. If you do get lost, you quickly realize it, and your intention will put you back on your path.

Without an intention it is easy to get distracted and wander aimlessly, living an unintentional life. When you have too many interests, and not enough time, things that are really important to you end up falling by the wayside.

The use of intentions was critical when I arrived in Florida, as this move involved several major life changes at once, bringing up a lot of fear and anxiety. Although I had an idea of what I wanted to do, I didn't have a plan to achieve it. I often felt aimless and scared. How was I going to support myself? What was I going to do? My mind wanted answers; I wanted assurance that I would be okay in the future. Understanding that energy follows attention, I knew if I wanted a life of support, joy, and peace, my thoughts and attention needed to focus in that direction.

As I faced my fears, I tried not to increase them with drama, stories, or projections of what might, or might not, happen. The practice of Witnessing, feeling pure sensations, and breathing helped me experience what was coming up, and allowed it to exist. Intentions gave me the direction to create the life I wanted. They allowed me to move into trust and faith, letting go of the need for security. This enabled me to enter the field of pure potential, where my future could be anything.

When faced with unlimited potential it is important to have some direction. If you are confused about what you want, "anything" can turn into "nothing." When you send messages of fear into the field of potential, you create a life filled with fear. Intentions were the main technique that helped me stay on track to create the life I wanted. They gave me the courage and trust to live in unknown territory.

TWO TYPES OF INTENTION

There are two types of intention: a primary intention that is your life mission statement, and a working intention that keeps you on track with your mission. The working intention may change over time, but it always supports your primary intention, which never changes.

Regardless of the type of intention, it must be expressed in the present tense, you must resonate with it, and it should be concise so you easily remember it in times of stress.

The reason to use present tense is that you are sending yourself, and the universe, a message. For example, you would not say, "I want to be at peace." Your higher self will hear "I want" and give you *wanting* peace. Because you phrased your intention with "to be," it will never be now. Your peace will stay in the future, where you can never experience it. You need to re-word the intention to sound something like "I am at peace with myself." (Present tense, and in the now.)

You must resonate with your intention because, if it feels like a lie, it will not work for you. If you have a lot of anger, making an intention of "I am at peace with myself" can feel like a stretch. Perhaps, "I accept my anger" might feel right. Or "I allow my anger to exist" might be more appropriate. As you allow and accept anger, it has nothing to push against; it has nothing to feed on, so the accepting will cause it to diminish.

Working intentions can change from day to day, or you may use the same one for some time, depending on your needs. The most important thing is that it continues to resonate with you. When it no longer works, see if you can tweak the wording. If not, perhaps you need to create a new intention.

Intentions are always about you; they help you change your perspective or attitude to accept the best from life, to create the best for yourself. If you feel unloved by your husband, your intention could be "I accept the love my husband has to offer me." You would NOT say, "My husband loves me a lot." That would be about him, rather than about you. You can only change yourself. By changing yourself, you will affect others, and perhaps they will change. Or perhaps not. That is out of your control.

Intentions are not the same as positive affirmations. The purpose of an intention is to help you relax with how life is now, while moving you in a set direction. For example, instead of "I am happy," you could phrase it "I accept my sadness." Another option could be "I experience greater peace and happiness in my life." Both statements help you be at ease with life as it is, yet move you in the direction of greater happiness. When you accept your sadness, it will start to move out, leaving room for happiness.

YOUR MISSION STATEMENT INTENTION

Your main intention, or life mission statement, is fixed. It never changes. You never arrive at it, but it keeps you moving in the right direction. Below is a formula developed by Kamani Desai for determining your main intention:

- Write down the names of four people you admire. They can be living or dead, you may personally know them, or know of them. For example, Mother Teresa, Martin Luther King, your second-grade reading teacher, your grandmother…

- Beside each name write down six characteristics or traits that person possesses.

- Look at all the words or traits you wrote for the people on your list. Count how many times each word or trait appears. For example: if you wrote "caring" for Mother Teresa, for your grandmother, and for your second-grade reading teacher, count that word three times.

- List, in order of frequency, the top five words or traits you wrote down.

- Now tweak each of your words so it resonates with you. For example, "compassionate" was your second-most listed trait. You resonate more with the word "loving." Go ahead and change "compassionate" to "loving."

- Plug in your top three or four words to fill in the two sentences below. One of the **words** will feel more right than the other words as you repeat the sentences to yourself. One of the **sentences** will feel more right than the other sentences as you repeat them.

  I. "I am here to be _____."

  2. "I am _____."

- Which sentence feels the best to you?

- Next, play with or tweak the sentence you chose until it resonates. If it is fine as it is, leave it. For example, I originally had "I am loving." However, I decided on "I am a powerful loving presence." I resonated with the words "powerful" and "presence" when I added them to my sentence.

Now you have your primary intention. When you face big decisions, repeat your intention to yourself. Does this decision align with your intention? When you take action, does it align with your mission? Your primary intention will keep you going in the right direction. If you become confused, look toward your mission statement.

WORKING INTENTIONS

Working intentions support your fixed main intention. They change according to circumstances, shifting with what you are going through, while remaining in alignment with your mission statement.

When I arrived in Florida after leaving my career, home, and husband, I often felt surrounded by infinite space with nothing behind or in front of me. As a result, most of my working intentions were along the lines of trust and faith. One favorite was, "I have complete trust and faith in the mysterious workings of my higher self." I wanted to attract the best possible life to myself, without the limitation of my rational mind. Otherwise, I would just go back to school and get a job, since that is what I knew how to do.

I wanted my life to be an expression of love and service to others, to teach others how to practice yoga off the mat. I didn't know how to do that in a way that would support me financially. I wanted to realize and express my highest potential, while living my best possible life. My rational mind didn't know what that was. My higher self did.

When I would get scared about my future, I would say my intention, feeling the trust and faith that all was fine. I could let the field of pure potential know what my highest desires were, and allow my higher self to decide how to achieve them.

"Everything in my life is for my highest good" was another intention I used frequently. This one helped me feel aligned with reality, and to trust that a power greater than my ego knew what was best for me. I could look back on my life and see situations that, at the time, frustrated me. Later I realized those were the best things that could have happened. This intention helped me stay on track, aligned with life and situations as they were. It helped me trust that what was before me was good for me, even if I didn't understand how.

Since I was not working, no longer had a career, and had no idea how I would support myself in the future, I used the intention "I accept the gifts of the universe." This gave me a sense of security. I also focused on prosperity and abundance throughout the day to reinforce this experience. If I found a penny on the ground, I would pick it up, thinking, "I am one cent more prosperous." If someone paid me five dollars for something, I would think, "I am five dollars wealthier." If my car needed a repair, and I had to spend $200, I would think, "Because I have $200, I can spend it on my car." I reframed my thoughts to align with prosperity thinking.

As a result of this prosperity alignment, I felt the abundance in my life, and enjoyed the security of having my needs met. When I needed something, the means to get it were available. This intention helped me have trust and faith that the universe would take care of me, and guide me in what to do.

The other intention I often used was, "I am at peace with myself as I am and with my life as it is." I chose this because I would find myself thinking, "I will be happy when I'm teaching more classes," "... when my book is published," "... when I'm making more money." I decided I needed something to help me be at peace right now. I needed to be happy with time to write, time to rest from the major changes that occurred, time to enjoy walks in the neighborhood. This working intention helped me experience peace and support in the present, not sometime in the future.

Intentions gave me the tools I needed in the present to manage my circumstances and move me in the direction of my main intention. I couldn't experience my main intention of being a powerful loving presence if I wasn't at peace with the "me" I was right then.

Life can throw some big stuff at us, making our main intention seem irrelevant to the moment. This main intention is quite general, setting an overall direction for one's life. I found tthe working intentions are more specific to the current situation while keeping you connected to your main intention. Working intentions keep you aligned with your main intention, while helping resolve the current troubling issue.

Remember: It is extremely important to express all intentions in the present tense. They must also resonate with you. You can play with some of these words that make good intentions: "accept," "trust," "realize," "faith," and "power." "I accept the abundance in my life." "I trust in the process of life." "I realize my power through the source within." Make up some of your own short sentences that resonate with you.

INTEGRATIVE RELAXATION METHOD

A technique that adds extra power to intentions is an integrative guided relaxation method, known as yoga *nidra*. You can download one for free at www.kenyongatlin.com/readergift

Yoga *nidra* takes you into a deep state of relaxation, while remaining awake. You reach this state every night in sleep, but you are unconscious, so you are not aware of it. In yoga *nidra*, you remain awake and aware, even though you are deeply relaxed and still. Your brain waves slow from the usual beta waves of the waking state to the slower alpha and theta waves of the sleep state. In deep states of yoga *nidra*, they slow even more, into the delta brain waves.

When the mind is in this slow, relaxed state, it is out of your way. It is so relaxed and still that it cannot dominate your subconscious energy, or block the super-conscious universal energy, known as God-conscious state. You now have access to where all of your pre-programmed habit patterns live. You also have access to the field of spiritual pure potential.

When you are asleep, you are not aware that you go to this place of silent emptiness. In yoga *nidra*, you are aware, able to make use of this super-conscious state while also addressing the issues in the subconscious.

In sleep and yoga *nidra*, you bypass the ego-mind that creates problems, going to the consciousness, or the Witness, that solves problems. Because you are aware in yoga *nidra*, you can bring this consciousness a problem to solve. Creating an intention using the instructions in the previous sections does this.

While in yoga *nidra*, you will be guided to silently repeat your intention a few times. Since the mind is too relaxed to interfere, your intention goes directly to your subconscious and super-conscious. During the day, when you find yourself in reaction, or in a stressful situation, silently repeat your intention and you will experience relief.

Often, when you say an affirmation or intention, your subconscious doesn't hear it. There is part of you that wants to change, and another part that is resistant to change. Yoga *nidra* is a way to bring all of you in harmony with what you want changed, which is why it is so effective. When every part of you integrates with your affirmation or intention, when you repeat it to yourself during the day, it has great impact, providing immediate relief.

When you are in yoga *nidra*, you connect to the Witness and watch everything that arises in your awareness. Sometimes pain, anger, or a past trauma might surface. Review it with detached awareness, like watching passing clouds. Whatever shows up in yoga *nidra*, is coming up to leave. Think of it like emptying a trash can. As you dump the trash, you see some of it as it falls out. Know that whatever surfaces, is on the way out. Just watch it from the distance of the Witness.

You might feel relaxed, a bit floaty, or dreamy, in yoga *nidra*. Or you may experience timelessness. A thirty-minute yoga *nidra* can feel like five or ten minutes. The facilitator's voice might sound far away, then close up, or sometimes disappear altogether. Whatever happens, just watch, and relax. There is nothing you need to do in yoga *nidra*.

If you are new to yoga *nidra*, when you first practice it, you will likely fall asleep because you become so relaxed. If this continues, when you lie down, bend one arm at the elbow so the forearm and hand points up. As you fall asleep, your arm will drop, waking you. If you are not comfortable lying down, you can sit in a chair instead. Do not lean back in the chair; remain upright, with your feet on the floor. If you feel comfortable lying down, practice that way, on the floor, or in bed. You might like a rolled up blanket or a bolster underneath your knees to support your back, with a folded blanket or pillow under the head. Relax your arms by your sides. Be comfortable, but do not fall asleep!

Once you are ready, play your guided yoga *nidra* recording. You can download one for free at www.kenyongatlin.com/readergift.

Working with intentions in yoga *nidra* has been, and continues to be, a powerful technique in helping me navigate life. Whenever you try to do something differently than you have always done it, you are in for a challenge. It is very hard to detach from the ego-mind, which is extremely uncomfortable with the unknown. Whether it is the unknown of a transition, or of responding differently to a situation, of breaking long-standing habits or even addictions, intentions and yoga *nidra* are a tremendous help.

Non-Attachment

THE FREEDOM OF NON-ATTACHMENT

Non-attachment is often thought of as a cold or heartless state of being. *Yet it is simply the absence of fear.* When you are attached to someone or something, there is an underlying fear of losing what you have. As you practice yoga to relax in each moment, you will discover you have fewer attachments to people and material goods. This is because the practice of relaxing reduces fear. You cannot be fearful and relaxed at the same time.

As you relax with each moment, you detach from your self-image and habit patterns, which are fear-based, so you can connect to the true source of love that you are. You actually have more compassion and right response to situations when you are non-attached, because your judgment isn't clouded in fears.

Life is full of changes, births, and deaths. The more attached you are, the more you try to manage what you ultimately cannot control. Where is the freedom or contentment in being afraid of losing something or someone? Where is the freedom in feeling you can't survive if you don't get what you want, or if you lose what you have?

When you lose something you're strongly attached to, you try to hang on mentally and emotionally. This keeps you from enjoying what life offers next. Life is like breath, flowing in and out, in a continuous cycle. When you experience non-attachment, you are in tune with the cycle of life.

Strong attachments can turn into obsessions, which may escalate into addictions. As fear lessens, attachments are reduced to preferences. Eventually, preferences reduce to non-attachment. No matter where you are on the attachment scale, as you continue to relax with life you automatically move toward non-attachment.

Preferences do not generate a strong fear of loss. When your preferences do not happen, you might be a little disappointed, but you will not suffer. The disappointment dissipates quickly and you are free to enjoy what comes next. Living with preferences is very freeing, even though preferences are not the same as complete non-attachment.

Simply observing your attachments and feeling the sensations they create, while relaxing with the breath, is how you move toward non-attachment. You cannot practice non-attachment;

it simply happens as a result of practicing relaxing with what is right now. You will notice your attachments become fewer and less intense, and yourself feeling freer, as you practice relaxing with life.

As you move toward non-attachment, you move closer to the state of love. **Love is not fear-based, and attachment is not love.** True love is beyond ego-based fears and attachments. That is why it is unconditional. Through the practice of relaxing and accepting whatever each moment brings, you release your identification with the fear-based ego. You move toward unconditional, non-attached, universal love.

ACCEPTANCE

The practice of acceptance leads to non-attachment. We often think accepting something means liking it. In reality, acceptance is acknowledging what is before you as it is, without resistance. You can accept something, and still choose to change it. **When you change a situation from a place of acceptance, it is a responsive action.** When you make a change from resistance, it is a reaction. Reactions rarely, if ever, have lasting positive results.

Acceptance reduces your dislike and suffering, and begins to neutralize the situation, creating the possibility for change. If I ask you to come over to me, you can only come from where you are. Acceptance is recognizing where you are, which then allows you to move in the direction you choose.

Whatever life presents to you, when you accept it, you align with reality. When in alignment with reality, any changes you make will also be in alignment. Therefore, these changes will be effective. There is insight within the space of acceptance, which helps you see the root of the resistance.

When you make changes from the place of resistance and frustration, you only change the people and the scenery, while the same old issues and circumstances continue to arise in different disguises. When you do not accept what is before you, you are fighting with life. If you make life your opponent, it will be you who loses. You are not separate from life, so when you resist what is, your ego is fighting with reality, which creates a split between you and life. When you decide you are tired of resisting life and fighting with yourself, you are able to start practicing acceptance.

All of the practice techniques I have discussed in this book are integrative techniques that align you with life. As you practice them, you automatically become more accepting, at peace with what is before you.

When you accidently break your nicest wine glass, accept it. Feel the pure bodily sensation of frustration. Breathe, and watch your thoughts about the broken object with detachment. Nothing you do can bring the wine glass back, so practice opening your heart and mind to the situation. Be at peace with it.

Whatever has just occurred is not going to be different because you wish it had not happened. Did someone steal your wallet? Accept it by breathing, feeling, and Witnessing, what is occurring in your body. Notice the sensations subside, and yourself relaxing, as you come into alignment with what happened. Then make the phone calls to cancel your credit cards.

Wishing things didn't happen, or happened differently, means you are trying to live the impossible. No amount of mental complaining or frustration will change the situation.

Use your practice to accept whatever happens. After you accept, perhaps there is an action you can take to improve the situation. Perhaps not. Either way, you remove the fight, aligning with reality and life.

Once you stop resisting life, life stops resisting you. When I moved to Florida, I had to get a paper notarized at the bank. After I waited a good thirty minutes, the notary finally had time to see me. She looked over my paper and said there was no place specified for the notary stamp. She didn't think she could notarize my form.

While she checked with management, I realized there was nothing I could do. I would either get the paper notarized, or would have to make some phone calls and wait for a new form. As soon as I accepted the situation, my frustration left, although my preference remained. Because I accepted what was, if my preference did not happen, that would be okay. I would go through the necessary process.

Luckily, the notary was able to use a special stamp and I did not have to get a new form. I often find this is the case when I do not resist what is happening. It seems there is nothing for life to resist against, so situations tend to work out smoothly.

ACCEPTING YOURSELF

Everything comes from you. As you accept yourself, you will become more accepting of others. The key to accepting yourself is to Witness the aspects of yourself that you dislike. You cannot fight the ego with ego, you can only "starve" it through the Witness.

Anger, fear, frustration, and depression are manifestations of resisting life. When you wish that those parts of you did not exist, you add more resistance, fueling the behavior you are trying to change. What you resist persists.

Think of your strong emotions like a child crying out in pain. When you hold the child and care for her, the pain subsides. The child is at peace. When you abandon the child or fight with her, the child cries louder. Hold, and care for, your strong emotions from the Witness. Watch, and feel the pain dissipate.

Love is the solution to all of your problems. **Acceptance is the first step in learning how to love.** Give space to the parts of you that you hate. Let them exist, as you hold them in your awareness. Feel the pure sensations of these parts of you. Breathe deeply into the sensations. Recognize that they are there.

With your loving attention, anger, fear, and sadness cannot continue to exist.

POLARITY VS. CONFLICT

Life consists of opposites: inhale/exhale, day/night, high tide/low tide, hot/cold, ugly/pretty, pain/pleasure, calm/agitated, birth/death, and so forth. The opposites are complementary and interrelated when you do not choose one over the other. In fact, you cannot know one without the other.

If you never experienced hot, you would not recognize cold, as there would be nothing to compare. As soon as you decide cold is better than hot, or you like pretty and hate ugly, you have to control and manage how to keep what you like while avoiding what you don't like. You have created conflict where there is none.

When you learn to experience what is, as it is, without labeling it "good" or "bad," the conflict turns into polarity, complementary opposites that coexist. One is not set against the other. As non-attachment develops, you can be comfortable with fat *or* thin. Your experience of life becomes much more relaxed, because you live life without creating conflict.

The suffering we create starts with making a choice of like/dislike. Notice whenever you make a choice, and move toward choicelessness by breathing, and feeling pure sensations, from the perspective of the Witness. I am not talking about everyday functional choices such as should you buy the blue car or the red one, or should you eat on the patio or in the dining room. I'm talking about choices that have an emotional charge to them, even a slight one.

For example, at one point in my life I was living near someone I didn't like. When I saw him, I changed my route so I wouldn't have to walk by him. If I planned to have my lunch on the bench near the orange tree, and he was nearby, I found some other place to eat my lunch. This avoidance was a small drain on my energy that accumulated over time. By using the practice, I was able to neutralize my aversion progressively.

If there is someone you are attracted to, you spend extra energy figuring out how to see him more often. Attraction appears to feel better than aversion. Both drain energy while they pull you back and forth. Both have a cumulative effect of using your energy to push something away, or pull something to you.

I used to have arachnophobia, an extreme aversion to spiders. If I saw a spider nearby I felt a paralyzing fear. I've lived most of my life in Florida, where bugs and spiders are large and plentiful. I was always on alert for spiders. Entering a room, I would scan it before settling down. I would go camping, and always be on the lookout before going into the tent, sitting down, or reaching into my backpack. When I did see a spider, I had to find someone to remove it and "rescue" me.

It took a tremendous amount of extra energy to always have one eye on possible spiders, and if I found one, to get someone to catch it. If I didn't have such a strong dislike, I could have relaxed and enjoyed what I was doing, without constantly trying to avoid something.

I was well aware that my arachnophobia was creating conflict, yet for a long time I was helpless to change my reaction. As I've learned the practice of yoga off the mat, I have been able to apply it to my arachnophobia, and have slowly gotten over it. An unrelated event further cured my fear. I talk about that later in this book. Practicing integration with everything in life can affect areas you were not even working with.

ATTACHED TO THE FAMILIAR

I notice that I'm quite attached to many things, the familiar being one of them. Over the years, my heart had been pulling at me to pursue a career more in line with my yoga practice, yet I had no idea what that career would be. The desire to leave my fabric design career, and do something with yoga, was growing stronger every day. I began to feel suffocated by my job, even though there were parts of it I still enjoyed. Circumstances finally helped me leave the familiar routine of the job that I was attached to, yet at the same time, wanted to let go of.

Although I could sense that life was moving me out of my career, I still had to make a conscious decision to leave. I felt a strong pull to take a leap of faith and resign, yet I had fears about the uncertainty of what to do once I left. I had no plan for my next career. I felt I needed time and space to figure that out. Leaving the work force was the only way I would get the space I needed. Witnessing gave me the courage to take that leap of faith to leave the familiar.

Once I arrived in Florida, and had nothing much to do, I realized the fast pace of the past eight years had become embedded in my body and energy. I had an attachment to always having something to do, to being extremely busy, to having a routine, a schedule to keep. Suddenly none of that was in my life. There was nowhere I had to be, and nothing I had to do. On one hand, I was grateful. On the other, I felt scared and confused. Because I could detach from my thoughts and identity around this issue, I could notice these feelings.

I would feel the sensations of being antsy and restless; surely, I should be doing something. What was I forgetting? My body and mind were used to being in motion, to being efficient. In the past when I would relax, it was within a set schedule, for a specific amount of time. Now I could do nothing for as long as I wanted. That sounded nice. It felt terrible!

To help me release some of this built-up momentum, I would take long walks, or go to the gym. I created a schedule of gentle "doing" to ease me into the abyss of no schedule or routine. I would make a "to-do list" of activities; take a walk, sit on the patio for an hour, vacuum the living room, or read chapters six through ten in a novel. Over the months, the momentum and restlessness cycled out, the dreams of working at my old job dissipated. I could feel myself coming into balance.

With each passing month, the momentum of the previous eight years was leaving my body and psyche. It took about seven months of relaxing with my discomfort to release all the effects. I compare it to steering a large ship. I had been steaming along in a particular direction, but had to slow way down before I could turn in a new direction.

LETTING GO

Over the years as I've practiced relaxing and experiencing non-attachment, I notice how much more I enjoy life. I don't hold on so tightly. Everything around me has more freedom and flow, including myself. I am freer to just live life and enjoy it. Practicing these integrative techniques with the losses in my life has helped me experience them and let go more easily.

Events, people, and situations always change. When you try to hold on to something that is ending, you only create tension and stress. When you let go of resistance to what is happening, what is ending is not as painful. Often that loss turns out to be a gain.

Due to the downturn in the textile industry, I was often changing jobs and relocating. I made major moves, buying and selling homes three times within a ten-year period. Each time was a practice in letting go of the home I enjoyed, my friends, and the job I was comfortable doing.

When my sister married and had children, I had to let go of the way our relationship used to be. She was now busy with her family. Although we remained close, the dynamics of our relationship changed.

All these external changes, losses, and gains are common. Although they can be difficult to accept and release, they help prepare you for the letting go of your internal concepts and beliefs about yourself. Many of your beliefs are embedded in the subconscious, where they are hard to access. Yet they create undercurrents in your life, such as a subconscious belief that you don't deserve wealth. No matter what you do to make money, you find yourself poor.

Because these are unconscious beliefs, they are the hardest things to release. Even beliefs that you know do not serve you, are hard to let go of because they are familiar, and in that respect, comfort you. Although it is a challenge to release these beliefs, through the practice of Witnessing and relaxing with what arises, you can do so within a short time.

I believed I wasn't good enough. That self-concept drove me to overachieve and overperform. I got a lot done, achieving external successes because of that self-concept. Society supports this common self-belief, since all bosses want their employees to get a lot of work done. I did not even realize I had that self-concept until I became so exhausted with overachieving that I had to stop.

As I let go, leaving tasks undone, or not taking care of other necessities, I felt extremely uncomfortable. I experienced sensations of burning and constriction. Sometimes I felt panic. Everyone would realize I wasn't good enough since I wasn't taking care of everything. The energy in my body was screaming at me to get something done. I allowed myself to experience this from the Witness, and felt the discomfort.

Through the process of letting go, not overachieving, and just allowing myself to experience the sensations, I released the belief that I wasn't good enough. Initially I felt confused as I let go of who I thought I was. However, once I made the shift, I noticed getting things done came from a peaceful place, rather than a need to prove my self-worth. I noticed others stepped up, empowered to act in the void I left for them to fill. I felt more balanced in my life, and regained my vitality.

GIVE UP HOPE

Pema Chodron writes about giving up hope. At the time I read that, I didn't fully understand. Hope seems like such a nice, positive, encouraging quality. Our society is very supportive of cultivating hope. While I was getting my house ready to put on the market, friends and family hoped it would sell. When my dad was in the hospital, people hoped he would get better and come home. During my career change, friends and family hoped I would be successful at supporting myself. I hoped for all these to happen, too.

During all this hoping, I realized how negative it was. When I hoped my dad would come home from the hospital, it was because I was afraid he might not. The people who hoped my house would sell were afraid it might not. When my parents hoped I would make money to support myself, they were afraid I might not. All this hope felt so negative.

That's when I realized hope comes from fear. It is a rejection of the present moment; it is about wanting something to be different or better. It is saying life is not okay; I am scared or worried, about me, about you. I noticed that when I hoped for something, it was because I was worried or afraid. When friends and family hoped for me, I felt their rejection of what was occurring in the present. I felt the fear for my future. I felt the pressure in hope to make things better somehow.

Everything has to go through its process. My dad could not get out of the hospital immediately. My house could not sell immediately. I could not support myself immediately. The pressure of hope hinders the process that life situations must go through. It is tempting to do something—anything—when you and others are hoping. But acting in fear creates fearful results.

I did this to my husband during his illness. We both hoped he would get better. I believe now that this just put pressure on him to try to get better faster, because we didn't want to accept the current situation. We were both frustrated, and hoping was making us more frustrated. Hope added fear, worry, and pressure to his illness. Hope is the same as saying your life is not okay because you are ill, out of money, or have a house you can't sell.

When you want to make changes for your future, you can only make them in the present. Since hope is a rejection of the present, it strips you of the power to make changes so things can be different. With hope, I felt confused, worried, and powerless. I find that when I just relax with the situation, and accept, I become more creative, empowered to make decisions and changes.

MESSAGES FROM LIFE

Life is constantly communicating with you through events and people. As you continue to relax and cultivate a degree of non-attachment, you are able to listen to life's messages and act on them. You can take care of situations while they are small and manageable, instead of waiting until you are in a crisis before paying attention.

At one point early on in my practice, I was insanely busy, working full time with a two-hour round-trip commute, finishing up an extensive yoga-teacher training program, teaching three yoga classes a week, planning a wedding, fixing up a house to sell, and looking for a place to live when my job relocated. I was completely overwhelmed and exhausted.

As I drove to and from work on steep, winding mountain roads, I would find myself wishing to be in a car wreck. Not one so bad that it killed me, just bad enough that I could be hospitalized and get some rest!

One day during this time, a police officer pulled me over for making an illegal U-turn. Luckily, he only gave me a warning instead of a ticket. I did not think too much about it until the following week, when I was pulled over again, for speeding. Once more, I only received a warning. This time I thought about the meaning of these two incidents. I had not been pulled over in ten years. Suddenly, within one week I received two warnings from the police. Both had to do with me being in a hurry. I thought, "Maybe life is telling me to slow down." I figured I had better listen, or I might get into an accident and end up in the hospital for real.

Soon after, I talked to my boss, which resulted in me working from home one day a week until the company relocated. My fiancé took over some of the wedding planning. We also decided to stop looking for a house to buy. Instead, I rented an apartment for six months, once the company moved. Although I was still very busy, it was now manageable. Interestingly, I have not been pulled over since, and I did not end up in the hospital. So I know I read the message correctly.

Life is always giving us messages about our life situations, pointing us in a specific direction. As you accept what is before you, you are able to listen and respond to those messages so you can align with life, and be in its flow. Acceptance helps you quickly determine if you are moving with life, or if you are resisting life and need to make an adjustment.

FLOWING WITH LIFE

As you release your attachment and hold on things, you are able to discern the flow of life. It requires paying attention and consciously relaxing with what is before you. Resistance and tension blocks life, keeping you from the support and flow life offers.

When I want to check out the flow of life, I take action to initiate an idea or desire. Then I watch and feel what happens next. I could not move to Florida, or quit my job, until my house sold. I worked hard to make it look appealing so it would have a good chance of selling. Then I let go, waiting to see what would happen. When it sold within eight weeks, I knew I was going with the flow.

When I resigned from my job, my employer accepted my two-week notice and paid my vacation for the following year. That was very generous, way beyond what most companies would have done. Again, I knew I was supported and in the flow with transitioning to Florida.

There is still effort when you go with flow, but no struggle. There is support along the way, and situations tend to work out, even if it's not how you expect. If you feel stuck, the practice of relaxing will allow inspiration to come so you can adjust the situation.

There have been occasions when I've received no inspiration other than the feeling that I should wait. At the time, waiting did not feel like flow or inspiration to me. In hindsight, staying with my "stuck" situation was exactly what I needed. As I learned the life lessons of patience and commitment, the situation changed, and I flowed to the next lesson.

10

Becoming Fearless

PURIFICATION

In yoga there is a practice called *tapas*. Frequently this is translated as "discipline." The true meaning of *tapas* is "to burn." Burning is a purification process. It takes discipline to stay with it because it is quite uncomfortable! When you have a reaction to someone or something, there are uncomfortable sensations in the body, which is why you want to escape. Nevertheless, the burn of feeling your fear, anger, or sadness is what removes it. When you go through the fire, you are becoming free of that emotion. To stay with the sensations from your reaction, you must have discipline to feel the heat and pressure.

Burning and purification are like a lump of coal, that when subjected to heat and pressure, becomes a clear diamond. When you stay with the discomfort of the burn, using your practice to watch and feel the burn, you clear out your emotional and psychological baggage. You become cleaner, and clearer, from the inside out. Knowing this helps you to be willing to go through *tapas*. You are becoming a clear, beautiful, strong diamond!

All fires burn out. When you stay with the burn, it escalates, growing uncomfortably hot. Finally, it dissipates, and you feel the cooling and peace. The fire of *tapas* burns out your unresolved past that created the reaction. Eventually, you do not experience as much fear or anger with situations that used to trigger those emotions.

Similar to how a fever kills germs, *tapas* kills the emotional and psychological "germs" causing your suffering. Once free of the source of pain, you experience life more fully, with joy. It is also like undergoing surgery—painful during the process, but after healing, you are free and clear to enjoy your life. So, when you experience the burning of being present with anger, fear, or sadness, know that you are in the process of becoming free of your reactions.

You need do nothing with this process except watch and experience it. The practice that brings up the cause of suffering is the same practice that clears it out. Whenever some emotion comes up—anger, fear, or sadness—connect to the Witness and watch. This gives you some distance so you can stay with the sensations of burning away what you no longer need.

FEAR

Fear has been with me throughout my life. I used to be shy, afraid to speak up or be noticed; afraid I would not be good enough, or afraid I would fail. I was born with this fear. When I was only five or six years old, I would worry about how to buy groceries, balance a checkbook, or get from point A to point B in the city. I would see my parents do these necessary tasks, and worry that I wouldn't be able to take care of myself. My mom assured me I would learn when I was older. I was not able to trust that, so I continued to live in fear and worry.

I wouldn't let that stop me though, so most people did not know I had so much fear. I learned to suppress it, pushing it into the background so I could still function and do the task before me. Fear even motivated me to excel at what I did, so I could avoid failure.

Since I had suppressed fear throughout my life, that is what came up for release. The more I learned to relax, the more fear I was able to release. Here is my account of how I handled fear when I moved to Florida and how I stayed with fear as it cleared out.

I naively thought that after I arrived in Florida and rested for a couple of months, I'd get busy with the next thing in life, such as preparing to go back to school or teaching a lot of yoga classes. I was wrong. The next thing turned out to be nothing! It didn't feel right to go back to school, and no one was hiring yoga teachers except for one nearby place, where I taught two small classes once a week. I felt suspended in nothingness. Behind me was a past that no longer existed. Before me was nothing! As it turns out, nothing is exactly what I needed.

Although I left my past behind, I was so busy with moving out of North Carolina that I hadn't fully processed what happened. I was too busy and overwhelmed to experience the emotional effects of the loss of my career, home, and husband. Although I did my best to relax and experience as much as I could at that time, I also suppressed a lot. After I moved to Florida, I had the time and space to be with whatever arose, which was fear, doubt, and sadness, for a good six months. I could experience and process what I could not fully experience the year I left North Carolina.

My entire life (until I moved back in with my parents), had been very structured—going to school, getting a degree, and working for companies. I was always fulfilling someone else's agenda while working on my own agenda part-time, on the side. For the first time in forty-two years, there was no one else's agenda before mine. What lay in the future? What do I do next? I had a few ideas but didn't know what to do with them.

I frequently went to a nearby yoga *ashram* so I could be in touch with the spiritual teachings, receiving reminders that this discomfort and fear would pass. I did deep breathing and inspirational reading. I reminded myself of everything that was good in my life, and how grateful I was for caring parents who were able to support me. I reminded myself of well-known people, who have gone through similar life-changing transitions. These thoughts would remind me that starting life over is not uncommon, and that you can succeed at following your heart, even if you are not sure what that entails.

GOING THROUGH FIRE (TAPAS)

After several months of consciously relaxing with fear, my practice ignited the fire to burn a lot of it out. When suppressed emotions are released, you experience them on their way out. I was emptying my garbage, watching it leave.

One morning, I awoke in the grips of fear. I was so scared I didn't want to get out of bed; I could feel my pounding heart, my increased blood pressure. My chest felt constricted, there was a constant knot in my stomach, and my throat was tight. Sometimes my hands trembled. I felt nauseated and could not eat much. I was terrified of nothing in particular. My teacher, Amrit Desai, had talked about this, so I knew it was coming up in order to leave. Nevertheless, the intensity surprised me.

The fear was so great it physically hurt me. I wished for the relief of when my life would be over. Since I was well-practiced at Witnessing, I could observe this and create some space between me, the fear, and the pain. I could create space between me and the thought that I didn't want to live. I would sit on my parents' patio, staring into space as I felt the sensations and thoughts of fear. Since I could Witness this, on some level I knew I was not my fear.

Even while I felt the pain of fear, I could sense an underlying peace. The fear ebbed and flowed. Sometimes it stayed for a while. Eventually it would dissipate and release. One moment it would be strong, the next it would weaken. I knew all this pain was coming up to go away, which helped me stay with it.

Witnessing kept me from becoming paralyzed when the fear grew intense. I connected to my breath, and went on long walks in the sun, while feeling the sensations of walking. I drank a lot of water, which helps flush out hormonal toxins created from fear, anger, and stress. I turned to nature and inspirational reading. I maintained my formal practice, as it helped to release the emotion, providing some relief. I did everything I knew how to do, every technique I have written about in these pages.

All of my practices helped me stay with the intensity of the fear. I'd be lying if I didn't tell you I was extremely miserable at this time, while my practice was burning this fear out of me. I was grateful my parents were traveling out of the country and did not have to see me, as I did not need anyone to "fix me" or stop this process. I did, however, need the support of understanding people, as I could not do this completely on my own. I went to my teacher's yoga *ashram* several times during this period so I could receive support from others who knew what I was going through, and who could encourage me to stay with the process. They did not try to make the pain go away, as they knew they couldn't.

After about six weeks, the intensity abated. Although there was still some lingering fear smoldering away, I could feel it slowly dissolve over the next months. The waves of fear and anxiety were smaller, further apart. In place of the fear was a sense of adventure and wonder about what would be next.

In the quieter space of awe and possibility, I could connect with my heart and inner wisdom, allowing myself to be guided into the next thing. I could follow my own ideas, as well as suggestions from others that felt right, as I put one foot in front of the other. I knew where I wanted to go, but I couldn't see very far along the path. So I slowly walked in the correct direction, using intentions as my compass.

For several months, this was a process of moving forward, and then stopping in fear. Even when I stopped, I was able to stay on my path, just hanging out with fear. It would dissipate. I would continue forward again. After a while, I experienced more peace. I felt much more comfortable with the unknown, more confident in moving forward. I felt free, able to go where guided, without worrying how it would all work out.

A little over a year after the above experience, I had another intense, paralyzing experience with fear moving out. Thankfully, it only lasted several hours instead of six weeks! I was in a yoga-training course, working on a presentation for evaluation. I chose to teach on the topic of resistance since I had a lot of personal experience using these techniques to work through resistance.

I organized my notes and thoughts, but felt such a tremendous amount of resistance and fear arise that I couldn't put together my presentation. I had nothing prepared after working for three hours. For the first time in my life I thought I'd have to tell the teacher I would not be showing up for my presentation, because I could not prepare one.

The terror I felt had no particular source. In desperation, I shot off a prayer for help. About five minutes later, a friend I was thinking I really needed to talk to, came up the stairs as I headed down. After talking, crying, and processing through the strong sensations of fear, they suddenly left. It felt like an entity left my body. Although I was drained and tired, I also felt light and free. The fear and resistance were gone, and I easily worked on my presentation.

Whenever you suppress or avoid something, it is submerged, energetically absorbed into your body. In order for it to leave, it has to come back up. When people leave a room, you see them go out the door. When fear, anger, sadness, or any other emotion leaves, you feel it and watch it go. It is not always an intense experience; sometimes you hardly notice. Other times it is very intense.

In the early summer of 2012, I went through another period of fear arising on a consistent basis. I would wake up feeling fear, experiencing constriction in my gut and heart. I would be in the middle of a beautiful day with nothing upsetting me. Suddenly, I would be scared. When these sensations arose, I placed my left hand over my heart and my right hand over my belly, where the sensations were the strongest. I would feel the tingling in my hands and think of divine energy pouring through them into the sensations. I would breathe, relax, and say to myself, "I allow these sensations to exist as they are." This helped me open and soften into the fear, allowing it to release and move out.

For my whole life, I suppressed fear without even knowing it. I did this automatically, so I could move through the situations in my life and take care of what needed to be done. I operated the only way I knew how, so I could have the courage to do what I was afraid of doing. Since I always did this, it was my "normal." I didn't know there was another way to feel and *be* in life. I never even realized I was anxious, I felt how I always felt. When my consciousness brought light to this area, the light started to burn the fear out.

Amrit Desai would sometimes say, "The door you are trying to shut is the door to your freedom." As I went through the door of fear, I became free of fear. This is not a one-time process. Every time the door opens, I walk through it. When fear arises, I relax with it. I notice it becomes less intense and comes up less often. I always feel lighter and permanently less fearful after the sensations pass.

After going through this process, I realized how anxious I used to be. With the experience of no anxiety for the first time in my life, I had something to compare to my past feelings. My normal was shifting as I was relaxing with life.

When you go through the fire of *tapas*, it is important to know it will not kill you. It is killing what doesn't serve you. When you rid yourself of what holds you back, you will feel much better. This practice releases the submerged pain and emotions, allowing you to get through the process.

You have to go through the sensations. You cannot go around them. Just walk right into them. Feel what arises from the Witness. Breathe and relax with the sensations as the process releases what you have avoided in the past.

The more you can relax with the discomfort of *tapas*, the quicker it will move through. Many times, I resisted the sensations, creating more misery for myself. I was uncomfortable with the burn, yet when I would try to get away, I felt suffocated by the process that had begun. When I just relaxed with it, the process moved discomfort out faster. I was freer, sooner.

RELEASING IDENTIFICATION
FROM THE EGO

The ego is based in fear and the urge for survival. The ego has desires. It grasps at things, gives you the promise that if you get what you want, you will be happy and content. But you never are for long, because the ego always has more desires. One house leads to a bigger house, leads to two houses, three houses, a private jet, a higher salary, a better job, two TVs, fifty pairs of shoes. Whatever you get, it is never enough, because it is based in fear, which can never provide more than temporary happiness.

As you apply your practice, you diminish the ego and move closer to spirit. You become more content with what you have, and need less to be happy. You are connected to the never-ending source rather than the fear-based ego.

The ego is not a bad thing. The problem lies in identifying with your ego and believing you are your self-image. By using these yoga practices, you maintain the ego so you can function in the world, but you identify with your soul. When you connect to your true self, to your soul, you see your ego and self-image for the mask that it is. You are able to use your self-image to help you function in the world, while all along knowing you are the embodied soul.

My teacher often refers to spiritual practice as a cross. There is the horizontal line of the time bound worldly ego, and the upward, timeless vertical line of spiritual practice. This creates the cross. Many people do not fully commit to a spiritual practice because at some point they experience the pain of the cross. The pain of sacrificing the self-image. It is a type of death. Because of this, you eventually need a teacher who knows the way, as well as the support of others who also practice.

It is worth releasing some of your ego so you can enjoy the freedom and peace of spirit. The ego is a false identity that stands in the way of your soul. Keep your ego because it serves a worldly function, while knowing it is not your true identity. **You are the one that has an ego, you are not the ego.**

The ego tends to have a bad reputation, especially in spiritual teachings and literature. It is important to understand there is nothing wrong with ego. In fact, if you are to live in the world, the ego has an important function. The ego motivates you to stay alive and participate in the world. Use your ego to be in the world. Know that you are the soul within.

One time, as I was listening to a teaching about the cross, I saw a vision of my ego as a character clawing and grasping at the story it built for itself. It was like those cartoons where the character runs off a cliff and tries to scramble back to the ground behind him, only to realize it is too late, and he falls.

My ego had an image of "I'm incapable" and "I can't do this." As I've continued practicing with speaking up, standing my ground, and feeling all sensations so I can be comfortable with conflict and others' reactions, my ego's story became more and more invalid. I could not believe my self-image anymore. The story was dying; my ego was losing ground. Of course, I'm still identified with my ego, but less so every day.

Chapter

11

Following Life

THE PATH OF THE UNKNOWN

It has been an adventure following where Life leads me, rather than making plans. I have always done this to a degree, but never to the extent as I've done since moving out of North Carolina. My mind wants to know "What is next? How will it work out?" These unknowns can cause fear to reappear, creating unpleasant sensations.

When I Witness my mind trying to figure out the unknown, I disengage. As I withdraw from the fear-creating thoughts, focusing on pure sensations, the fear dissipates, and I dismantle my reaction to the unknown future. This allows me to go where Life leads, instead of where my ego demands. As I relax with the unknown, I've noticed my clarity and intuition get stronger, which makes it more obvious what to do next, and where to go.

Following Life is a much easier way to live, as there is no struggle living *with* Life. The struggle is in resisting Life and ignoring its guidance. Living *with* Life is like living with a powerful, always protective, best friend. You can just relax, ready to do the next thing when it presents itself.

Spirit is a quiet voice. Often, the ego voice is too loud and noisy for you to hear spirit's communication. You cannot hear or sense anything when bombarded with constant mental noise. Through practice, your mind becomes quieter, relaxed, and alert. You are then able to hear the wisdom of your higher consciousness so that you can follow where Life leads.

When you let Life show you the way, you get the fulfillment from living that you want, rather than the promise of fulfillment that ego makes. You may think you reach fulfillment when you have the large house, the pair of shoes you saw in the store, the promotion, or a new car. But look at all the rich and famous people, who have everything money can buy twice over, yet still feel unfulfilled and miserable. Their sadness and misery are all over the media.

Ego demands that you strive, struggle, and control, to get what you want. Life allows you to relax and follow, giving you what you need for fulfillment. A sure way to do this is to have a consistent practice that allows you to hear Life's messages. That gives you the strength and courage to follow the guidance received. As you become clear and learn to listen, you can even ask Life questions and you will get answers.

Sometimes I'll ask while journaling. I'll write down my question to Life. As I get the answer, I write that down. I did this often during my first year in Florida, going through my transition. Every time I asked, the answers that came forth during this period were to do nothing, just allow. What? How could there be nothing for me to do?

There was a particular situation causing me frustration because it wasn't moving along as quickly as I wanted. I was feeling impatient, wanting to do something about it. One morning I asked Life, "What can I do to make this situation move faster?" The following is the answer I received: "Do not go to all the trouble of climbing the tree to pick unripe fruit. It will not taste good. Wait at the bottom of the tree for the ripe fruit to drop. Then you can pick it up and eat it. It will taste wonderful and you can enjoy it." Once again, do nothing, just wait and allow.

This is the beauty of practice, and of becoming best friends with Life. You become clearer to receive answers from wisdom. With clarity, if there is something to do, you will know it, and it will not be a struggle. There will be an effortless ease to it. Many answers and moments of inspiration will just present themselves, without any effort on your part. When I feel impatient about something, I remind myself not to pick unripe fruit. Let flowers bloom in their own time, when they are ready.

LEAP OF FAITH

It is easy to say you have faith; it is a different matter to act in faith. Faith is moving into unknown territory, trusting that you are supported. Faith is not blind; it is built on understanding and experience, through study and practice. I have faith in my practice because I have experienced the results. Before you can take leaps of faith, you take steps of faith. Those steps give you the experience to take the leaps.

With every step or leap, faith grows, and you are able to move further into unknown territory. It took a leap of faith to resign from my job and move to Florida. I had no idea what was going to come next, and no plans. As I've used this practice to face my fears of the unknown, and have experienced support, my faith has grown.

I'm sure there are times in your life you thought were disastrous. In retrospect, they turned out to be the best things that ever happened. Faith is realizing at the time something occurs, that it is the best direction, whether you think it is or not; that there is a higher order to Life that the ego-mind cannot grasp. The ego wants to figure everything out. Faith says there is nothing to figure out; all will work out when it is time.

As I live more and more in faith, I can relax and be happy in each moment, as there is nothing to worry about in the present. This has been the result of the practice for me. As I study, gaining understanding and experiences from my practice, I trust the practice. This trust grows into deeper and deeper levels of faith.

As you open yourself to Life's possibilities, you are sometimes guided to act against your family or cultural conditioning in steps and leaps of faith. One such incident happened when I decided to withdraw a portion of my Roth IRA. My parents had conditioned me to save, and never touch my retirement money. This was deeply ingrained in me, so I never considered that money as available. My other savings were dwindling. I only had several thousand dollars left. I would have to get some sort of part-time job.

Although I don't mind working, something didn't feel right about that choice. It felt like getting a job would not support my intention of teaching yoga, or of being of service to others in some capacity. It would also be difficult to take the advanced teacher-trainings I wanted to take. I badly wanted to take those trainings, but how was I going to pay for them without a job? And how would I have the time if I had a job?

I continued to pray about this, meditating, and mulling it over. I felt the sensations that arose with the different scenarios I considered. The only solution that felt right was when I thought about withdrawing money from my IRA. My mind really did not like this idea. It took several weeks of breathing with this, relaxing, and feeling the sensations below the thought-induced emotions, before I was ready to make that withdrawal.

I felt strongly that I needed to invest in myself, now, rather than later; that it was important to take those yoga trainings and this was the only way I could pay for them. I was breaking through a very strong paradigm from my upbringing.

When I finally withdrew the money, I actually felt relieved. My body told me I made the right decision. I was excited about going back to school! Yoga school, that is, which was not a school my family, or most of society, would consider a good investment. But it was the school I knew was right for me. Although I didn't realize it at the time, I was also giving the Universe a strong message that I wanted to do this, even at the risk of shifting out of my comfort zone.

Since it was so ingrained in me to leave that money untouched, it was a sacrifice to go against that. God accepted my sacrifice, and opportunities for advanced trainings I hadn't even considered began to show up. I even landed a part-time job at my teacher's yoga *ashram*, so I could make some money while immersing myself in the teachings at the same time! I didn't look for this job, or apply for it. I was simply asked if I would accept it.

THE PRACTICE OF SELFLESS SERVICE

When I moved in with my parents in 2011, life kept guiding me toward yoga. I found myself drawn to the practice of *seva* at the *ashram* of my teacher, *Yogi* Amrit Desai. *Seva* means selfless service; serving while expecting nothing in return.

This is a practice of *karma* yoga.

Karma means action. Your actions create a cycle of cause and effect, which causes more action—or *karma*. If you are completely selfless, and expect nothing, your actions do not create any more *karma*. *Seva* has shown me how selfish I am, and how unselfish I can be.

I would practice *seva* in the kitchen during programs—wash dishes, chop vegetables, set the meals out in the dining room, whatever was needed. My day would start at 5:30 am and finish at 10:00 pm. I would do this for several days in a row, go home, and sleep for several days to recover. The grueling kitchen schedule created a constant shortage of help. However, I found working there to be an interesting combination of exhaustion, misery, fun, contentment, and the joy of an open heart. The latter is what kept me going back.

I also found the kitchen a powerful place to practice and grow. I would conduct *seva* experiments with myself. I stood for hours at the sink washing dishes. My legs would ache, my back would hurt, and I would be exhausted. I'd focus my mind on the rhythm of the dishwashing, the pure sensations in my body, not on the achy label or story I attached to them. I'd focus on my gratitude for these teachings, and for the people there to learn these teachings. I would often find myself energized by focusing on the present moment, and on gratitude.

The power of my mind, and what I chose to focus on, had a huge effect on my energy level and on how my body felt. I would still be tired after a couple days, but my mind could greatly influence how I felt about that. I discovered I could feel exhausted, yet joyful, still be able to serve. There were other times I would simply be exhausted, and absolutely could not serve any longer.

I grew by pushing to the extremes of my edges and beyond, using the practice to back off if I was way over my edge. I used the practice to determine if I was really over my edge, or if I could disengage from my mental complaining and sensation-labeling to return to my edge. Could I tap into heartfelt joy regardless of what I was doing or how long I was doing it?

I learned to manage my energy and take care of myself by using these techniques of staying present and breathing. I discovered that talking and having "fun" could sap my energy if I was already exhausted and I needed that energy to chop vegetables. I learned how to cultivate joy and contentment while working. I learned how to say, "Enough, I'm done." I was able to practice with these extreme conditions because I knew that after several days I'd be going home for a while and would not be back for another four to eight weeks. *Seva* in the *ashram* kitchen was like signing up for practice boot camp!

MOVING INTO THE YOGA *ASHRAM*

I never considered living at the *ashram*, though I was practicing *seva* often. I thought moving into an *ashram* would be giving up, escaping from life. I would be hiding from the world. My rational mind would not let me move there, so it did not happen until I surrendered and had enough trust and faith to follow higher guidance. It felt very much like following, as there was hardly any effort on my part to make this move.

Near the end of my first year practicing *seva*, I was asked to fill a kitchen assistant job during *ashram* programs. I wasn't sure I wanted to do that. After I talked with the *ashram's* administrative director, I agreed to try it out, assisting only during programs.

During my first program as kitchen assistant, I sat in the meditation room on a break, and looked up at the picture of *Yogi* Desai's *guru*. As I gazed at the picture, I had a sudden thought. "You need to move here." That took me by surprise and scared me for a moment. I worried about my two cats, and about how I would make money if I lived there. Immediately I had another thought, "Don't worry, everything will work out." I knew those were not "my" thoughts and I had to act on them. Everything worked out, more perfectly than anything I could have planned. Within weeks I moved into the *ashram* with my two outdoor cats.

At the *ashram*, I have been able to support the needs of the community. The community has been able to support my need for spiritual transformation. I am immersed in these yoga teachings, learning from a yoga master every day! Although I never would have planned to move here, due to my preconceived ideas about living in an *ashram*, I am glad I listened to Life and followed. It took trust in God and Life to follow where my mind didn't want me to go, but where my heart knew was right.

The purpose of an *ashram* is transformation. Transformation is a process of dis-identifying with the ego and self-image, and identifying with the silent source that we all are. It has not been an easy or comfortable process for me, especially in the beginning. In fact, the first year of my experience at the *ashram* felt like surgery. It was very intense, even painful. As I removed what didn't serve me, I experienced more inner calm and peace.

GURU

Gu means dark, *ru* means light. A *guru* is someone who shines the light of wisdom into the darkness of unconsciousness, so you can see your own light and inner *guru*. Most of us don't realize we have an inner *guru*, our own guiding light, to show us the way. Having a practice turns on the light of consciousness so you can connect to your inner *guru*, which will lead you to an outer *guru*. Both are necessary for spiritual growth. The outer *guru* helps you stay on the path, and further develops your connection to the inner *guru.* This reminds me of another definition of *guru* I like: Gee U Are U.

I met my *guru* in 2004. At the time, I did not know he was to be my *guru.* That didn't happen until seven years later. The concept of having a *guru* was foreign to me. I didn't think it was healthy to blindly follow someone, or worship them. *Gurus* were for lost, flakey people, not people with jobs or an education! At least, that was the stereotype I believed.

I first met *Yogi* Desai, or Gurudev, at a workshop in an *ashram* in Virginia. He began talking about yoga teachings, religious teachings, and life. I was mesmerized. I never before heard someone with so much wisdom explain these teachings with such clarity. It was the first time I heard someone speak the truth about the meaning of life while providing the tools to access this meaning. For the first time, someone explained spiritual practice in a practical, useful way I could implement in my daily life. Even so, there was still no way I was going to have a *guru.* But I *could* have a teacher.

For the next seven years, I traveled to see him periodically. I regularly practiced his teachings. I bought his lectures and practice CDs, and listened to them often. Although I would have liked to see him more often, there were too many obstacles. In retrospect, this was necessary for my growth. I had to rely more on myself, and use the teachings in my everyday life, since I couldn't be physically near him. This developed my own inner strength and self-reliance.

The teachings were my support, not the teacher himself. The teacher became my support *through* the teachings and practice. As I practiced and listened to him, my understanding and experience grew. My own light began to shine brighter. I felt more connected to him and the teachings with every passing year. I was realizing, more and more, how effective and powerful the practice was as I moved through life.

I began to realize that trusting and having faith in someone is surrendering your ego and self-image, so your own light can shine through. For me, it took seven years to trust him deeply enough to surrender and accept him as my *guru*. It was a slow, steady process. When I made the decision to be his disciple, it was one I could trust, knowing it was right for me.

Once I made that commitment and surrendered, I noticed that my practice deepened at a quicker pace. The need to be disciplined about it decreased, and my practice came more from a place of devotion.

Gurus are not necessarily perfect. In fact, they are quite human. However, they are able to keep their light shining, and show you your inner light. They are traveling the path they are teaching. *Gurus* are just further along the journey than you are, so they can point out the obstacles. The *guru/* disciple relationship is one you need to enter consciously, because you must be able to trust before you can surrender. Your level of surrender will correspond to your level of trust.

If you surrender to someone unconsciously, you could put yourself in danger with an unwise choice. I needed to observe *Yogi* Desai as my teacher, and practice his teachings for seven years, before I could trust enough to surrender to a *guru*, to trust that I would not be led astray by him, or by myself. I needed to strengthen my inner *guru* with the teachings before I could surrender to an outer *guru*. A good sign you have chosen the right *guru* is that your own light and inner strength increases, not your dependence on another person. Gurudev has shown me who I really am, so I can progressively let go of who I am not.

Chapter
12

Skill in Action

ACTING FROM CONSCIOUS AWARENESS

The definition of yoga according to the Bhagavad Gita is "skill in action." This skill comes from conscious awareness rather than just honing a skill set. The more you identify with your soul and conscious awareness, the more skillful all your actions become, in every moment of your life.

Living at the yoga *ashram* provides many opportunities to practice skill in action. I learn how to get along with a variety of people in the community. It is not possible to avoid people I don't get along with, since we all live together. I therefore use the practice to be at peace with whomever I am with, and whatever I am doing.

As I often work in areas I have no training or skill for, I work on my edge. Through conscious awareness, and relaxing with the moment, I move beyond my boundaries. I learn to act skillfully through being present, rather than through learned skills. Since the daily routine constantly changes, I am not able to settle in my ways. The environment here is more unpredictable than anywhere else I have lived.

Ego likes comfort and control. With the constant changes of community life, the ego has a hard time. As soon as I gain a skill or grow comfortable with a job, I am switched to a different job. I must connect to the practice and relax, or I will be too uncomfortable to stay here.

My first job at the *ashram* was in the kitchen. I had never worked in the food industry before. My cooking experience was limited to preparing meals for immediate family and close friends. The hours were long, and the daily routine changed according to the guests' program schedule.

In addition to the constantly changing routine, I had to get used to people continuously coming and going. I never knew who I would be sharing my room with, or how many people would stay in the house with me. Within this seeming chaos was the support of a practice, teachings, a *guru*, and a community.

At the age of forty-two, it was a challenge to get used to this way of life. I had become accustomed to the routine and structure of my past life, with a job, husband, and home. Until I came to the *ashram*, I never realized how much I was able to control circumstances to support my habits and comfort. With the constant change at the *ashram*, I was in the perfect place to learn skill in action and break my habit patterns.

SELF-OBSERVATION

Earlier in this book, I gave the example of a mall directory to describe the Witness. That is what self-observation does: it shows you where you are so you can make the changes to move in the direction you want to go.

If you do not observe yourself, see your faults, and accept them, how would you ever change? You must see what you are doing if there is any hope of doing something differently.

It is important to be non-judgmental when observing yourself, otherwise what you see will not be a catalyst for change. When you judge and reject yourself, you feed your ego, not your soul, which keeps you from moving in the direction of your true self. Paying attention to your judgments and criticisms keep you attached to your self-image. It will keep you from the Witness, who simply illuminates where you are. When you find you are judging what you notice about yourself, withdraw from that thought. Let it recede into the background as you stop feeding that thought with energy.

The ego is not capable of dis-identifying with itself, and judgment is a function of the ego. When you judge and criticize yourself, you are trying to get rid of the ego *with* ego. That is impossible. It only increases your suffering.

When you connect to the Witness as you observe yourself, you are using who you are to dis-identify with who you are not. Judgments will be present, yet when observed from the Witness, you are not as caught in your self-judgments. They begin to diminish.

As you observe your faults, breathe, and feel pure sensation through the Witness. Every time you find your thoughts are judgmental, withdraw from them. Eventually your judgment will diminish. You will become more accepting of yourself, just as you are. This is how you develop compassion for yourself as well as others.

Some faults I have noticed about myself, that I have been overcoming are: being too nice at the expense of supporting myself, overworking to prove I'm good enough, taking responsibility for others' reactions to what I say or do, not speaking up, and shying away from leadership responsibilities for fear of failing.

I don't work on these all at once, I simply notice they are tendencies I have. When it is appropriate to the moment, I use the practice to overcome them and act more skillfully. Following are some accounts of how I've used this practice to work on myself.

ON MY EDGE AT THE *ASHRAM*

Within several days of moving into the *ashram*, I had the opportunity to speak up and let go of another's reaction to me. I lived in a three-bedroom house, and one of the housemates was a guy who liked me. Another woman at the *ashram* tried to convince me to "live a little" and enter an intimate relationship with him. Part of me thought, maybe she was right. Still, I sensed this would create unwanted trouble, distraction, and drama. I also sensed a psychological imbalance in him, due to the attachment he formed in such a short time.

After several days of his escalating attention, I decided to have a conversation with him. I told him I only wanted to be friends, nothing more; I did not come to the *ashram* to be distracted with a relationship, and he needed to move out of the house because it was awkward living together. (His original plan, before I arrived, was to move into his friend's house, and it was now time for him to do so.)

It was a challenge for me to speak up and clearly communicate my wants and needs. In the past, I wouldn't have wanted to hurt his feelings, and would have come across as wishy-washy. My communication would have been confusing, due to my desire not to hurt him, and I would have hurt myself instead.

Toward the end of the conversation I was tempted to tell him I was sorry, to soften the blow, but I wasn't sorry at all, so I refrained from the old habit. It empowered me to see how much strength my practice had given me. I was able to communicate clearly, regardless of his reaction and hurt. However, the lesson was not over for me.

He said he would honor my wishes; that he wanted to be my friend, felt deeply hurt, and needed some space. He isolated himself for a couple of days before I saw him again.

After he re-emerged we tried to be friends, but it was awkward. I knew he still really liked me, but it felt draining to be around him. I had to be careful of everything I did or said so he wouldn't misinterpret it.

I could see he was going through a lot of pain. Anything I said to try to be supportive only made the situation worse. This was hard for me, as I don't like to see people hurt, and I felt responsible for his suffering. Yet the best thing I could do to help him was to leave him alone.

The insight from my practice, and the opportunity to discuss this with a friend who also has a committed practice, helped me to know that this person's reaction was not about me, but about what I triggered in him. My lack of response to his affections brought up his own issues for him to Witness. My reaction, of wanting to help alleviate his suffering, was about me, and was my issue.

No one is responsible for another's reaction, yet I felt responsible for his reaction. Witnessing his suffering, Witnessing my desire to help, and relaxing with not interfering was a tremendous practice and area of growth for me.

Through the Witness, I allowed myself to feel the urge of saying or doing something kind. I felt the burn of not acting on the urge. I felt my pain in watching him suffer, and the pain of being helpless to alleviate it. I connected to my breath to relax with myself, and with the situation.

One morning I woke up early and felt lightness, clearing, and release in the air around me. I immediately knew the guy who liked me had left the *ashram*. Sure enough, at lunch, the administrator announced that he left during the night and would not be back.

For me, this lesson was an amazing testament to the strength of the practice, the power of energy, and a validation of my increasing intuition. The ability to know, feel, and sense is available to everyone. We are usually not quiet, or still enough, to feel and sense what is there. As you practice, you realize there is much more to life than what you see, hear, or smell.

It is energy that guides and animates your life. As you become quiet and centered, you will know things energetically before they manifest on the physical plane. You can guide your life from this energetic knowing, just as I avoided a messy relationship when I intuitively recognized that a psychological imbalance was involved. In avoiding the relationship, I worked through some of my discomfort around pleasing people and feeling responsible for others' reactions. In relaxing with the situation, I felt less responsible for his reaction.

SPEAKING UP

Communication is part of every interaction I have with others. I had to speak up for myself during my encounter with the housemate. Clear communication is how I express my needs in supporting myself, and how I teach a yoga class. If I don't speak up, I won't be able to work on any of the other areas I have observed about myself. Therefore, I work on this all the time, because opportunities occur all the time.

One regular opportunity I had was during Gurudev's morning teachings. Gurudev would teach for about an hour in the mornings before inviting us to share our experiences, ask questions, or share our insights from his teachings. We would speak into a microphone because all these sessions were recorded. Since my practice was to speak up, I almost always shared despite my discomfort. Even if I wasn't sure what to ask or share, I opened my mouth, hoping something came out. It always did.

Many times all I could do was cry into the mic and choke out a few unintelligible sentences. I've even done this in front of large groups of people. It didn't matter what I said. What mattered was that I shared into a mic, before a group of people. Over time, this has gotten easier. I rarely get overwhelmed or cry anymore. My communication and understanding have grown clearer. I am more comfortable with speaking up.

NOT REACTING TO OTHERS' REACTIONS

As I mentioned in a previous account, I have often felt responsible for others' reactions. If I said or did something, and someone became upset or angry, I felt I caused that emotion. This kept me from speaking up or saying what I thought was important. I used to censor what I said or did, based on how I thought others would react, because I didn't want them to be upset with me. This behavior felt like a prison, as I was not free to say and do what the moment called for. I have worked to overcome this behavior, especially since I arrived at the *ashram*. I have consciously applied the practice of Witnessing, feeling, and breathing, whenever I felt responsible for someone else's reaction.

Immediately after the incident with the male housemate, the universe brought me the perfect person for learning the above lesson. Tim used to be one of the program chefs. He would sometimes stay for a couple of days before and after programs before heading home. He and I got along well before I moved to the *ashram* and accepted a position as kitchen assistant.

In my new position, I needed to communicate procedures to him, which created some conflict. For a good two or three months, everything I said to Tim, unless I asked him to show me how to do something, got a strong reaction. At first I thought, "What is wrong with me? Is it my tone of voice? The way I'm saying things?" After I talked to several people about this, I realized everyone had the same issue with him. It wasn't personal, or how I came across. Nevertheless, I was definitely reacting to his reaction, and felt uncomfortable anytime I had to tell him something.

My old issue of feeling responsible for others' reactions stared me in the face every day! I was either going to work through this, or be so uncomfortable with the frequency of his reactions I would end up leaving. I chose to work through it and break free of the restraint this issue had over me.

Since we worked long hours together, I had ample opportunity to practice. I would say something and he would react. Then I would concentrate on my breath, Witness, and feel the pure bodily sensations beyond the thoughts about the feelings. As I did this over and over, I started to notice I felt more at peace with his reactions. I could say what I needed to say and not be so concerned about how he received it.

Since I no longer reacted to him so strongly, I noticed he was taking responsibility for his own reactions, and more often working through them. We were the perfect match, able to support each other in our practice and growth.

Although I worked on this issue frequently while working with Tim, I consciously practiced it with everyone when appropriate. One time, a program participant had a cup of tea in the meditation room. To keep that room clean, one of the *ashram* rules is that no food or open containers with liquid are allowed. Normally, I wouldn't have said anything to the student because I would have worried how she would react to the request to remove her tea. Since I was working with this area of my life, I reminded her of the rule, and the reason for it. She very agreeably removed her tea from the room.

Another time, a student started to set up his cushion for the program session before we were ready to have students get their belongings situated. I didn't think twice about asking him to wait ten more minutes, as we weren't ready.

These examples might sound trivial, but when you work through your issues that cause reactions, small or trivial is where you want to start. Remember, lift small weights before lifting big weights. Anything bigger would have been over my edge, where I would not have been able to productively practice and work through my issues. As I have practiced in this way with others' reactions, it has gotten progressively easier for me to just say and do what the moment calls for, without concern about the reactions of others. This has been very freeing for me, worth the discomfort of practicing on my edge.

OVERWORKING

Another of my unconscious past behaviors has been to overwork. This stemmed from a feeling of inadequacy. I felt that if I did a lot, and did it well, I would be accepted. I did not realize the extent of this tendency until I moved to the *ashram*.

When I was a textile designer, I made it a point to leave at the end of the scheduled workday, so I thought I had balanced behavior regarding work. Looking back, I realize I had stopped at the end of the workday so I could teach yoga classes, cook, and eat a late dinner with my husband before getting ready for bed. I still worked long days; I was just not designing fabric the whole time.

When I moved to the yoga *ashram*, I noticed my driving desire to do a good job, which seemed to come from a fear of failure. I realized this mindset had been with me all along, an underlying fear of failure that pushed me into overworking in order to be successful. Now that this had been illuminated, I could make adjustments to achieve a more peaceful balance.

Since the purpose of an *ashram* is spiritual transformation, events seem to happen that you are either willing to face and work through, or you will be so frustrated you leave. I got my opportunity to notice this issue of overworking while I prepared for the first program of the year.

This program was a large event for the *ashram*. We expected 135 people the first night. I was new in the kitchen position, and of course, wanted to do a good job. At 8:30 am, the chef rushed in and started to tell me everything that needed to be done. I hadn't even finished my breakfast yet. She wasn't due in for another hour! I raced around, getting items together for her, while I tried to finish eating. Some of the volunteers that were supposed to help canceled at the last minute. So it was just the chef and me until 1:00 pm trying to prepare dinner for all those people.

It would have been acceptable to cook something simple. The chef wanted to make bread, pies, and some other fancy dishes, even though our help had canceled. I realized she had the same issue I had. At 1:00 pm someone finally showed up to help. A couple hours later, someone else arrived.

By that time, I was completely frazzled. At one point, the chef told me to empty the rice cooker and put the rice into a covered tray. I said, "Okay" and went over to the rice cooker. I stared into space with no clue why I stood there. I asked the chef, "Did you just ask me to do something?" I knew I was far over my edge, so I said, "I'll be back," and walked out of the kitchen amidst the frantic chaos. It was hard for me. I felt I had failed. I couldn't function anymore and had no choice but to leave.

I walked to the lake, where a friend joined me, offering comfort. She helped me see the craziness of the situation, and my issue of overworking in an effort to prove my worth. She pointed out that if circumstances hadn't forced me to take a break I wouldn't have noticed this about myself.

After an hour of talking with her, breathing, and feeling the sensations subside in my body, I was ready to go back to the kitchen. I was much calmer, centered, and able to slow down and be helpful. We served up good food, and I learned something valuable about myself.

I also learned it is impossible to practice when you are way over your edge. I could not use the practice to center myself because I was too caught in the chaos of the moment. When you get past your edge, you enter flight or fight mode, and you can do nothing else. I had been fighting; then I switched to flight. I had to get away to calm down. Once I centered myself, I could go back and work on my edge, where practice is productive. I could use the practice to stay centered even though I returned to the same situation.

With practice and experience I've learned to be balanced with work. I can still do a lot of work; now it is less from fear of failure. The work is more from a natural response to the moment rather than from a need to prove something. Of course, this is all a progression. It took more than this one incident to learn my lesson. I still experience fear of failure, but it is less frequent, and I am more relaxed with it.

LEADERSHIP POSITIONS

In the past, I have preferred support roles, working so others can do well. This is due to my fear of failure. My initial reaction to responsibility is, "OMG, I don't think I can do this. I don't want to be in a role where people depend on me. I might make mistakes or be unable to solve problems." The interesting thing is that I always do a very good job, and am very responsible and dependable. So most people don't realize I have an initial reaction of not being capable of doing a job. Still, my successes have stemmed from a fear of failure rather than from a relaxed response to the moment.

My first leadership position was my last job in textiles. I thought I had been hired as a designer. Although I knew I was to help the other designers in the studio, I was told that the line director would be the ultimate go-to person if I needed help. Once I started working there, I quickly realized I was the go-to person. If I didn't know how to do something I would have to learn. When my business cards came in a month later, my job title was Senior Designer. I hadn't signed up for this! I thought I hired in as a designer.

The universe gives you what you need. I needed to be a leader to learn that I was capable. I was often out of my comfort zone that first year as senior designer. Still, I solved problems, helped the other designers, and became a good go-to person. My practice helped me *be* with my discomfort and detach from it. The breathing, feeling, and Witnessing, allowed me to relax with leadership and problem solving. My practice helped move me into responsibility, strength, and power. By the time I left that position, I had confidence in my ability to solve problems and to share that knowledge with others.

As I have used my practice in various situations, I have been able to relax more with the needs of the moment, and to determine what those needs are. I "act more skillfully" when I am at ease. With all of the challenges I've worked through, I go to my edge; that place that is uncomfortable, but not *extremely* so. I breathe with the discomfort, especially focusing on the pause at the top and bottom of the breath. I Witness my discomfort, and I feel the pure sensations of the experience—the biological sensations beyond the thought-induced sensations.

Soon I feel more relaxed with the discomfort, and it goes away. I grow, and find it easier the next time to speak up, or not react to others' reactions. I find it easier to balance work and take a break. I find it easier to support myself, and to avoid being too nice to others at my own expense. It is all a progression; none of this happens overnight. One day I realized, "Wow! I'm not anxious about sharing anymore. And I don't feel so guilty taking time off work."

Before you can be comfortable, you have to be willing to be consciously uncomfortable. Your unconsciousness creates discomfort all the time. When you consciously experience your discomfort, at least you are working it out. One day you are free of it.

CORPSE POSE OFF THE MAT

Savasana, or the Corpse Pose, is done at the end of almost all yoga classes. In this resting pose, you lie on your back for five to fifteen minutes. The name is appropriate because you are as relaxed and still as a corpse. Its purpose is to allow the body and psyche to integrate and balance all the work you did during the class or practice.

In the Amrit Method of yoga, an integration period is done after each pose. The first half of the pose involves effort, as you hold the pose and relax with the building sensations of energy. The second half is when you release the pose, and bring awareness to the increased energy and sensations flooding through your body. This second half of each pose, and the corpse pose at the end of practice, integrate and balance the energy. This combination of effort and rest makes the pose and practice more effective.

I was surprised to experience the power of this integrative rest period in my daily life after moving to the *ashram*. Between taking programs, working programs, and living in the *ashram* community, I was often practicing on my edge. I was holding the pose of "life situations."

Several months into the year, I began to notice my greatest growth came after I had periods of rest away from the *ashram*. I would go through a challenging situation, and then spend several days away from the *ashram*. When I would come back to the very same situation, I would notice something had shifted within me, and it was no longer a problem. I discovered I naturally acted more skillfully in the situation after these periods of integration.

At first, this surprised me, since I was only resting, not practicing with the particular situation. I was not consciously taking time off to integrate, I was simply tired and needed to rest.

After a while, I made the connection, and realized the rest periods integrated the work I had done in the life situation.

The combination of using my practice to relax with the situation, then getting away for a break, was the same as holding a pose and then releasing the pose; it was the same as doing Corpse Pose after a long sequence of active poses. This combination of activity and rest were necessary in completing the integration process.

Chapter 13

Willpower and Surrender

FINDING BALANCE

Both willpower and surrender are necessary to achieve balance. The power of will gives support to surrender. Without this support, surrender becomes weak, as when someone acts like a doormat, allowing everyone to step on her. Willpower by itself becomes aggression, like the person who bulldozes over everyone to get her way. Neither extreme is healthy.

Willpower provides backbone to the submissive person. Surrender provides softness to the aggressive person. Both are needed to receive and give direction. I'll give an example of what happened when I surrendered to a situation I was trying to control with my willpower.

When I planned to move to the *ashram*, I worried about my cats, especially Taz. He got into fights whenever he stayed out all night, and I often had to take him to the vet the next day. Because of this, I would keep him in at night, letting him out only during the day.

At the *ashram*, he would have to be outside all the time. Therefore, I brought a large kennel cage with me and planned to keep Taz in the cage at night. I knew he didn't like going in the cage, but I was worried about his safety.

The fourth night, when I locked him in the cage he looked depressed. I felt bad for him as I walked back to the house. Once I got to the house and started to wash the dinner dishes, I had a sudden realization: "Those are not your cats to lock up." At that moment, I knew I needed to surrender my will. I went outside, and opened the cage.

Once I surrendered, and let God and life take care of my cats, I felt free of worry. I am not the owner of anything; I am just in charge of caring for people, animals, and things for an undetermined amount of time.

Both of my cats have done well and are the happiest they have ever been. They have even been helpful to all the people who came to the kitchen during programs. When those people went through trying times, they often went outside, and felt soothed by petting my cats. My cats seemed to know when someone was out of sorts and needing some kitty love. They served the programs and *ashram* needs in their own way.

None of this could have happened if I stayed in control and refused to surrender to the situation. Being in co-creation with life provided better care for my cats than I ever could.

ACCESSING WILLPOWER

I used to be out of balance with willpower. When I found myself in a conflict with another person, I tended to surrender to their will in order to keep the peace. If I disagreed with someone, I kept quiet, and went along with his preferences. The times that I held to my will, it was usually in a passive-aggressive manner. I did not have a healthy relationship with willpower.

When faced with conflict or resistance, I felt constriction in the pit of my stomach, which immediately closed off my chest and throat. I felt a strong desire to flee and hide, which caused me to suppress my true feeling, so I could move through the situation. On the outside, I appeared confident and competent, while inside I was tied in a knot.

At the *ashram*, I consciously worked on this issue. During an advanced teacher-training program, a couple of experiences gave me insight into this, helping me resolve it faster.

During one of the days of this training, I did some breathing exercises combining sound with focusing on the abdomen, which is the power center in the body. Once I felt relaxed, I did a martial arts exercise where you make fists, tuck your elbows into your sides, and make a strong punch with the right arm, saying, "Ha!" You repeat this, alternating your arms. This exercise activates the abdominal power center in a relaxed, yet forceful, way. Next, I did the same punching exercise with the word NO!

After practicing for awhile, I partnered up. Person A stood still and looked person B in the eyes. Person B did the martial arts exercise, punching and shouting "NO!" while facing their partner. "NO! NO! NO!" When it was my turn to punch, and yell "NO!" I felt like throwing up. That overwhelming constriction in the pit of my gut was rising. I felt hot and shaky. I was crying, and I wanted to run away! I calmed myself, and repeated the NO exercises until I could do them without feeling sick. After the training, I worked with them on my own, incorporating them into my morning practice for a couple of weeks.

On another day during this training, I was placed with a small group of participants to do some role-playing on conflict by enacting scenarios that might happen while teaching. When it was my turn, I knew the enactment would be one of the group members being antagonistic toward me. As soon we began the role-play I felt my belly constrict and move up toward my throat. I felt myself energetically close off; I suppressed the sensations as best I could so I could respond to the exercise.

I thought, "Wow! I know I'm not upset at my group member because he is doing what he is supposed to do, just playing the role." At that point, I realized it was the sensations in my body that I wanted to avoid. It was not about the conflict or the external situation.

My resistance to conflict was never about the situation or the other person; it was about how uncomfortable I felt. Conflict would arise. My desire to flee would be so strong, and the sensations so uncomfortable, that I wanted to avoid their cause. I would make things as perfect as possible to avoid upsetting anyone, so that I didn't have to feel uncomfortable. I had a facade of control and confidence; inside I was tense and tied in knots because I was afraid people would get upset with me.

It was hard for me to see what was happening because my need to be perfect only showed up in circumstances where conflict with another person was possible. If there was a possibility of resistance or conflict with someone, I would suppress my feelings so I could fix the situation to alleviate the sensations in my body. I was not conscious of this for a long time, so I couldn't work on this effectively. Going through the willpower exercises in a safe environment brought it to my awareness. Using the practice gave me the insight and the tools to stop suppressing the sensations.

My growth in embracing willpower was tested almost immediately. The evening following the training, I had dinner with my parents. The conversation turned to what I was doing at a yoga *ashram*. How was I going to support myself or save for retirement? They specifically asked if I withdrew any of my IRA money. In the past, I would have felt weak and wimpy standing up for something for which I didn't have conventional answers. I didn't know how I was going to support myself in the future. I did know that living in the *ashram*, immersed in these teachings while learning from a living master, was exactly what I needed to be doing for now. I could not explain how that would look regarding my future, or what I would do with this experience.

During this conversation, although I had no answers for my parents, I was able to stand in my power and speak with conviction, even though I didn't know how my life would turn out in the future. I really felt the power behind my words as I took my stand. My parents still worried, however, this time I felt they respected me for doing what I knew I had to do. I was amazed that I didn't feel too uncomfortable during this conversation of confrontation. Those exercises of NO, combined with feeling, breathing, and Witnessing, were paying off!

Just as I used intentions to accept and release my own feelings and sensations, I incorporated them to help me with others' reactions in conflict situations. I began to use the intention "I accept all sensations." I used this intention during yoga *nidras*, repeating it to myself when I was feeling uncomfortable in the midst of conflict. With this intention, I made quantum leaps regarding this issue.

I began to allow myself to experience the sensations I used to suppress. This allowed them to flow through me, becoming simple sensations, not good or bad. They lost their power over me. I could more comfortably hold the space for others' reactions, or feel relaxed with conflict. I could more effectively respond to the moment, or to the person in front of me, because I no longer feared how the sensations would make me feel when I spoke up.

COOKING FOR PROGRAMS

Sometimes life guides you where you don't want to go, but it turns out to be exactly what you need. When I moved to the *ashram*, my volunteer work in the kitchen became a paid position to assist the chef. During one program, my first summer at the *ashram*, no chef was available to cook. I asserted my will, asking the few other people who were qualified if they would cook for the program. No one was available except me. I really did not want to do this; if I didn't, the program participants would not eat. Life was guiding me to step up and cook for a program despite my efforts to avoid this. I know life has my highest interest in mind, so I surrendered.

The day the program started, I was nervous, but I had a good support team with me in the kitchen, and preparing food and cooking has a soothing effect. I discovered I could tap into the intuitive, creative aspect of cooking which kept me calm. I was able to stay in the moment, which helped me to relax with the cooking, and manage my team.

In life, no sooner do you gain confidence in what you are doing than life raises the bar. A couple of days after my success, the head chef resigned. The administrator approached me about becoming the official kitchen manager, in a paid staff position. This would be a more responsible and authoritative role than kitchen assistant.

The new position felt right in my heart, yet my ego-mind was worried. I had no kitchen experience or training other than that at the *ashram*. Every manager I had ever worked with, or known, was overworked and stressed out. What would I do to myself by taking a management position in an area where I had little experience? I was also rather uncomfortable with the title, money, and authority. Once again, my self-image questioned whether I was up to this job. I felt the incapable, inadequate me rise. The overachieving me stepped forward, wanting to take control to compensate for the feeling of inadequacy.

I knew I was at the *ashram* for training, and trusted this new position was the next step in my training. The role chose me, so I figured it was the right one for now. I trusted that God knew I was there for spiritual transformation. This must be what I needed, especially since I didn't ask for the position, and in a way, didn't want the job. In another way, I felt this was what I needed to do for my practice and spiritual growth. I also realized this position would help me with my continued practice regarding will and surrender.

MANAGING THE KITCHEN

I've described how, when I accepted the position as kitchen manager, I had no prior experience or knowledge of kitchens, cooking for large groups, or of managing. What served me were my established practice and an observant nature. I was willing to surrender to the unknown, opening myself to guidance. I had learned a lot about what worked, and didn't work, while assisting the two chefs during the previous year and a half.

The main thing that I knew did not work was the extremely long and labor-intensive days. The operational structure felt dysfunctional to me. Somehow, I needed to create some space to get a clearer picture of how to change it. I was too tired and overworked to have any clarity, other than to know that the setup wasn't working.

Although the spiritual practice is internal, there is nothing wrong with adjusting the external so you can continue the internal work. My discomfort was too extreme to continue practicing with my situation. I therefore removed a few responsibilities from the kitchen, and adjusted my hours so my days wouldn't be so extreme. This gave me some space to accept the situation, and to see how it could be different.

I talked to people who worked in other kitchens to learn how they operated. After several months of observing, and working within the current structure, it was time to exert my willpower and try some more changes.

I wanted the kitchen to have a structure that allowed for a balanced flow of operation. This was an *ashram* kitchen, so the people that came here were also engaged in a spiritual practice to transform their lives. The kitchen needed to be a place where we could practice, in addition to meeting the food requirements of the *ashram*. If you are way over your edge, exhausted, and stressed out, practice cannot happen.

I tried out a few different ideas, made adjustments and changes, finally settling on a system of two shifts, requiring two teams. This brought the workday from twelve hours to six hours, which seemed reasonable considering how labor-intensive kitchen work is. It allowed everyone on the teams to attend the morning practice, and every other day, to attend the teachings from Gurudev.

This system was much more balanced, which created a nice environment in which to work and practice. The volunteers started to enjoy being in the kitchen. It was no longer a place to avoid. I also made changes in between programs. I began rotating the *ashram* residents in to help make the midday meal. It was becoming a true community kitchen, a beautiful place to practice nourishing each other through food.

I realized changing the kitchen was like creating a living work of art. Being more relaxed, I would have an idea or inspiration to try something. I would try this, take away that, add this, make a tweak or small adjustment here or there. Before I knew it, I created a living sculpture or framework where people could flow in and out. It was a dynamic work of art, breathing and changing within the structure of operation, not unlike a dance.

Through observation and a willingness to try new things, along with a willingness to drop perfection, I was able to manage the kitchen. In managing the kitchen, I have transformed myself. In transforming myself, I have transformed the kitchen. This was possible through relaxing with how things were, in order to receive inspiration to make a change.

Often, in a *Zen-do*, or monastery, you are purposely placed in an area in which you have no expertise or experience. This puts you on your edge, giving you a lot to practice with mentally, emotionally, and physically. Although this isn't purposely done at this yoga *ashram*, it is what happened to me.

My work in the kitchen has been my greatest growth. Having a leadership role in an area where I had no experience or training pushed me to my limits, and often beyond. When I was way beyond my limits, I had to learn to get back to my edge. I learned how to use my practice to relax, observe, and feel what seemed right to try. It was an experiment in accepting the situation, willfully making changes, and continually finding the right balance between acceptance and change, between willpower and surrender.

ONE OF MY GREATEST TEACHERS

Tim, whom I mentioned earlier, was my greatest teacher in helping me access my willpower. Before I was asked to manage the kitchen, he had been trying to get a full-time job with the *ashram*. He used to own a restaurant, so believed he was the obvious choice. He was shocked to discover that I had been offered the job. This was a recipe for disaster.

He constantly told me I couldn't do the job because I had no restaurant experience. He rearranged everything in the pantry and the kitchen. He got mad every time I told him about a change or asked him to do something. I felt bullied by his comments, reactions, and presence. Every time I saw him, I felt my abdomen, chest, and throat constrict, and felt nauseated.

Gurudev says, "Everything comes from within. What you dislike in others, you dislike in yourself." He also says, "When you reject the external, you reject yourself." This truth was hard for me to swallow. However, I trusted Gurudev, and was willing to be open to the possibility of Tim representing what was in me. I was open to work on accepting Tim and the situation, as a way to accept myself.

The practice of acceptance helped me eventually see this truth. I started using the intention "I allow all sensations" to help me relax with the lead in my stomach, and the tightness in my chest and throat. Tim would say things referencing my inadequacy and lack of experience. I felt the sensations, connected to my breath and said my intention. This helped me stay present with how I felt. I consciously practiced relaxing with the feelings in my body without trying to push them away. I could feel the initial pain and constriction. As I relaxed, I could feel it travel up my torso and spread, before dissipating. I continually accepted how I felt with Tim, one moment at a time, by Witnessing my experience, feeling, and breathing, to relax with the painful sensations.

As I practiced breathing and relaxing with the waves of sensations, I was accepting what was in me. This was one of the most challenging situations for me to accept and to remain present. After about three weeks, I needed a break. I had to get away.

I left the kitchen for several days. In the space I created for myself, I could continue to relax with my feelings, nurturing myself with rest and time in nature. When I thought of Tim and my situation, I would allow the feelings and sensations to exist as they were. I didn't resist or suppress them. I used my practice tools at a safe distance from the situation. This helped me process without being over my edge.

The day I headed back to the *ashram*, I awoke with a feeling that everything was going to be okay. I felt I had been through a major trial and had come out the other side. Everything would be fine. When I thought of Tim and my situation, for the first time I felt neutral. There were no uncomfortable sensations in my body. The true test, of course, would be when I saw him.

To my amazement, when I interacted with Tim the next day, there was no external change to the situation, yet I didn't feel accosted. My internal reactions to him were greatly reduced. I could work with him without feeling attacked by his comments and reactions.

He would remind me of my lack of experience, and how I couldn't do the job, but it didn't matter as much. I was becoming free! It was as though I was a new me. I felt lighter in general, like a different person than I was in the previous three weeks.

I had completed the process of staying on the wave of sensation, and at the end of the wave, there was resolution and insight. By allowing myself to feel what I was experiencing while connecting to the Witness, I realized the truth of Gurudev's words. Tim's issues with his own inadequacy that caused him to be aggressive were the same issues in me that I expressed through submission. As I accepted the sensations, and relaxed with the painful experience, I accepted myself, and Tim. In this acceptance, I resolved my inadequacy and lack of willpower issues.

Over the course of the following several months, I still felt reactions and discomfort as I related to Tim, but less intensely. More and more, as time passed, I felt neutral. Tim turned out to be the perfect person to help me free myself from feelings of inadequacy and self-rejection. By accessing my willpower I could stay in the situation. By surrendering to the experience, I could use the situation to become free of my own physical and energetic pattern that had caused so much inner anxiety throughout my life.

PICTURES OF ME IN THE KITCHEN

Chapter 14

Transformation

IT TAKES A WARRIOR

The spiritual path is one of transformation from who you think you are to who you truly are. It is the path of the warrior. The battle you fight is with the ego. You cannot fight the ego *with* ego. The light of consciousness, or the Witness, is your main weapon. In yoga, you relax with this battle by using the Witness, breath, and the sensations you feel. Every stab or shot (reaction) the ego makes—feel it, breathe, Witness, and relax, to become victorious, to become more established in your identification with your soul.

As you can see by my experiences, while this path has not been easy or comfortable, it *has* been freeing. It is progressively easier, more enjoyable, and relaxing. I do not resist the process so much now, because I know there is peace and joy on the other side. As a result, I have since experienced tremendous freedom.

PAIN BODY

You spend your life trying to avoid pain, not knowing that facing it is the doorway to freedom. All of my small breakthroughs, and my major breakthrough with Tim, required me to relax with uncomfortable and painful sensations. That one experience was worth every felt sensation for the freedom I gained. I am now more free to experience peace no matter who I'm with, or what the situation. If I'm not experiencing peace, I know what to do.

I am reminded of Eckhart Tolle's description of the pain body; an energetic entity with which we unconsciously identify, sometimes described as our shadow-self. My situation with Tim kept my pain body active. My practice shined light on the aspect of my ego that was causing so much suffering. Just as paper will burn from the light focused through a magnifying glass, I burned away my pain body by using the light of consciousness.

I had been doing this with a variety of situations at the *ashram* and in my life, which continually lessened this pain body. The situation with Tim was so intense and constant that it finally burned that energetic entity out of me. It was as though I carried around a target that said "inadequate." He simply knew how to hit my target with tremendous accuracy. My practice shrunk my target so there was little for him, or anyone else, to hit.

It took deep trust, and commitment to the practice, to go through the suffering of that burning. The intensity was so great it felt like walking through fire. I wouldn't have been able to do it if I hadn't first practiced with easier, smaller situations. I had experienced a periodic jarring and loosening of my pain body throughout that year, until finally, one huge incident punched it out of me.

Knowing that the death of the pain body will not kill you helps you relax with the sensations of its dying. Breathing, and allowing the sensations to exist, allowed my pain body to leave. Releasing these pain bodies is the process of transforming from self-image to embodied soul.

I am grateful for my relationship with Tim. There had been times while working with him that I wished he would just go away. Had that happened, I wouldn't be who I am now. My relationship with him, and my practice, allowed me to dis-identify with my pain body, and realize the power and calm in the loving source that I am. That is why I consider him one of my greatest teachers.

Life always gives you experiences that move you in the direction of your soul, in the direction of divine love. These are often painful because we identify with our self-image, which resists this transition. I identified with my fears of failure and incapability. It was painful to face them. In doing so, and in choosing to stay with the practice, I was able to free myself, moving closer to my soul.

Gurudev taught me the practice techniques and gave me the support. Tim provided the opportunity to free myself. I say "opportunity" because I could have avoided the situation, remaining trapped in my self-image and pain. I could have chosen not to practice in the situation, and have asked to join the grounds crew to pull weeds instead, letting Tim run the kitchen. I am glad, however, that I surrendered to what was before me, trusting my practice.

THE EFFECTS OF DIS-IDENTIFYING WITH MY EGO

Letting go of my "inadequacy" self-image has transferred into many areas of my life that seemed unrelated, such as my arachnophobia. Two weeks after the intense experience with Tim, I saw a huge wolf spider, the size of my hand, in the hallway of the house where I lived. I was able to calmly trap it under a container and slide a paper underneath it, so I could release it outside.

In the past, I would not have been able to do that if you offered me a million dollars. I would have wanted the money, of course, but I physically would not have been able to get close enough, or be calm enough, to catch the spider. In fact, I would have moved out of the house, knowing spiders of that size lived there. I was shocked as I watched myself calmly catch this huge spider. There have been many incidents since where I have caught and released large spiders.

My arachnophobia is gone!

I also noticed a change the next time I visited my parents and interacted with my mom. Although I have a great relationship with both of my parents, in certain circumstances, I notice annoyance and an energetic charge with my mom. The first time I visited her after my transformation, she would say something and I would expect the usual charged feeling within myself. I found it was no longer there.

There were several occasions during that visit when I expected to feel my usual reaction, only to discover that I felt neutral. This was amazing to me! When my inadequacy pain body left, I began to experience freedom in so many seemingly unrelated areas.

Since my experience with Tim, I noticed I am not as anxious. As I prepared to cook for a major program, I felt no fear or anxiety. I did not overplan or overprepare in an effort to make everything perfect or to avoid any pitfalls. I felt comfortable just doing what was before me, relaxed and confident it would all be fine, whether it was perfect or not. This was an amazing freedom for me, and I can honestly say I enjoyed cooking for the program.

I have noticed I no longer overachieve as often. I'm still quite responsible and get plenty done. Now, my efforts don't come from a fear of failure. There is less drive behind the work. It feels more like working from a relaxed place, in response to what is before me. It is easier for me to cut back my hours without feeling guilty. I no longer feel like I have to control and manage in order to hold everything together. It strikes me that I am truly learning to relax with life, no matter how it shows up.

I did not realize the extent of my fears and anxieties until I released them. I had become used to them as an undercurrent in my life. They had been there for as long as I can remember, so I knew nothing different. Everyone has worries and anxieties. I could think of plenty of people who were much more fearful than I was. So if someone asked if I was frustrated or anxious, I honestly thought I wasn't. This was how I always felt.

Sometimes I would get a massage from a therapist who worked with meridian points and energy channels. There would be very tender areas in my body. He would ask if I was anxious, as those were points that related to that emotion. I wondered, "What is he talking about? I don't feel that anxious, especially considering all the change I've been through!" After my experience with Tim, I got another massage. This time those channels were not tender at all, which confirmed that I had released the anxiety not only from my psyche, but also from my physical body.

As I feel my way through pain and allow it to exist, I experience more and more freedom. I don't have to avoid pain, and therefore don't have to push anything away, or control anything. There is no need to avoid certain people, or to try to keep other people around, to make me feel good. I am free to come and go, to be with whatever or whoever shows up. When fear and anxiety arise, I know how to release them, and continue reducing my fears.

The title of my book is *Relax with Life*. When I chose that title, it wasn't because I was relaxed with life, rather because that was my intention. I wanted to head in that direction. I now see that this spiritual journey through yoga continually moves me into deeper levels of relaxation. As I become more relaxed with everything, I more skillfully respond to the moment. It is a continually unfolding process, as this doesn't happen only once.

THE SELF-IMAGE

It is important to realize you are not your self-image. Your self-image has changed over the course of your life. The way you think of yourself now is not the same as twenty years ago. If you are forty, you do not have the same self-image as when you were fifteen. There is an unchanging *true you* behind this shifting self-image; that part of you that does not change, but notices all the changes.

When you mistake your self-image for your identity, meaningful change is impossible; you are unable to move toward your true, loving self. You will not be able to experience the loss of your self-image. If you believe your very existence depends on your self-image, when it begins to change, you will feel that you are dying. Without knowing your true self, you would preserve your self-image at all costs, or adopt a new one.

The self-image does not care if it is positive or negative; it does not care if it is successful or a loser. It does not care if it is sweet and helpful, or mean and aggressive. The only thing the self-image cares about is that it does exist. When you completely identify with your self-image, you will never be able to go beyond it, even if it doesn't serve you well.

If I believe my existence depends on being incapable, then I subconsciously won't allow myself to be capable. If my self-image identifies with being a loser, I won't allow myself to be successful. Even though consciously I want to be capable and successful, subconsciously I won't be able to.

If you are incredibly successful, famous, and wealthy, what happens if you lose that? Who are you then? It is only when you identify yourself with the unchanging source, the embodied soul, that you can see your self-image for the mask it is. You remain unaffected, or at least less affected, by the changing situations of life. As you move toward your true self, you see the love behind all the masks, yours and others'.

As you identify with your true self, you identify with what is permanent. Otherwise, you will only trade in one self-image for another. You will continue to control and manage people, places, and things to maintain that new self-image. You are no closer to your true self.

Of course, you will still have a self-image. You need one to function; the problem is in mistaking your self-image for who you really are. When you identify with your true self instead, you can allow your self-image to become more transparent, and the loving source to shine through you. You become the *One* who has a self-image.

TRANSFORMING INTO FREEDOM AND EASE

After releasing a portion of my inadequacy self-image, the drive to overachieve decreased. I felt more desire to achieve balance in my day. Looking back on my life, I noticed the past twelve years had involved carrying heavy responsibilities. I took care of my husband while I worked full time and taught yoga. My transition from North Carolina to Florida involved a lot of work, and long days. When I moved in with my parents in 2011, I was too fearful and anxious to take full advantage of the respite. As soon as I moved to the *ashram*, working in the kitchen involved more hard work and long days. I learned a lot from all these experiences. They have transformed me into who I am today.

Caring for my husband transformed me into a more committed and steady person. The responsibility of managing the kitchen showed me the power within, and how to access it. While working and practicing in the kitchen, I learned to be more at peace with a variety of people and circumstances. I am less easily aggravated, and can more quickly drop my reactions.

I now desire to have shorter, easier days. Although I wanted this in the past, my need to prove myself drove me hard. Subconsciously I wasn't able to be easy on myself. That drive has diminished.

Gurudev once told me, "Even a good habit, if it becomes fixed is not good." This helped me immensely in letting go and leaving things undone so I could have some time for myself. My good habit was to have everything neat, clean, and orderly. When the garbage piled up, or dirty dishes remained in the sink, I would feel tense and do the chore myself. I started to relax with this feeling and allowed the situation to exist until it bothered someone else, or until I could assign someone to take care of it.

Finding peace with leaving things out of order gave me some time and space to take breaks, or to end my day before dinner. I took walks in the woods or enjoyed a swim in the lake. I relaxed with disorganization and with messiness. I still took care of my responsibilities. Now I included self-care in them. I found a cute little house I could afford very close to the *ashram*. Not on the community property, it allowed me some privacy, peace, and quiet.

LETTING GO OF THE KITCHEN

In the middle of my second year at the *ashram*, one of the staff members received a significant promotion. She soon began to manage and influence all areas of the *ashram*, including some of the responsibilities I had. She made decisions regarding the kitchen without consulting me or informing me of her plans. In the past, I would have felt devastated by this. I would have thought, "I'm a failure. I'm not doing a good enough job." Her behavior played into the power issues I had worked through in the last year; similar lessons from a different person.

This time around, I was pleased to notice her behavior did not bother me. I felt secure in my own power and could see this was not a reflection of me. Her behavior was simply her need to be in control. I was fine with her leaving me out of the loop. Less work for me to do! I was able to see this as a testament to my progress. Inadequacy was no longer an issue for me and she was there to show me that.

Within a couple of months, the administration transferred me to the office to work in admissions. I answered phones, talked to people about our programs, and took registrations, among a variety of other responsibilities. I sat in a chair, wore nicer clothes, and had shorter hours. Most of the time I even got weekends off. I no longer had a leadership position; I just did what I was told.

One of the residents asked what my new title was. I told her, "Ashvini." (That is my spiritual name I use at the *ashram*.) I felt fine with or without a title. I felt fine telling people what I needed them to do, or with being told what to do. It didn't matter anymore; these were just roles I played.

This is not to say there wasn't an adjustment period for me. As I settled into my new position in the office, I noticed many neglected tasks in the kitchen. I would hear complaints from our volunteers, and could feel the chaos in the environment. My mind wanted to create drama with this, to make up stories: "The place is falling apart. What is going to happen to the kitchen? How is the *ashram* going to run without structure and organization?"

All of those thoughts were fantasies that might, or might not, come true to some extent. They were also a distraction to avoid the discomfort of learning a new job. Sure, there was neglect in the kitchen, but I was also focused on that to feed my drama. There were things that were working well. I wasn't paying them any attention. As soon as I noticed myself caught in my drama, I withdrew from the thoughts, returning to my breath and bodily sensations. This allowed me to relax with what arose each moment and simply be with my discomfort.

The experience of managing the kitchen, and then letting it go, helped me realize that nothing of what I do is for results, other than the result of how I am being. As my actions reflect my being, it will naturally create results. Now, the kitchen is a reflection of someone else's being, with different results created. This has shown me that I don't ever have to do anything. I just have to be. The doing will take care of itself. With practice, I remember this more often.

Chapter

15

Expanding My Circle of Peace

THE CIRCLE

You probably have a small circle of peace, which means that many things outside that circle disturb you. The practice of consciously relaxing with disturbances is how your circle expands. You become comfortable with more people, places, and situations. Your experience in life is more peaceful as your circle expands to encompass more of what used to bother you.

For example, if you don't like to mow the lawn because you think it is a waste of time, that is a disturbance. Use that activity to increase the size of your circle of peace. Commit to mowing the lawn every week. Each time you feel frustrated or impatient with it, connect to your breath, with the motion of walking up and down the lawn, the sensations of your hands on the mower. Consciously relax with mowing the lawn. You will notice your attitude beginning to change. Before long, mowing will be included in your circle of peace. If you always avoid what you don't want to do, your circle of peace will stay very small.

As you do this with everything just outside your circle of comfort and peace, your circle will grow. Do not practice this with irritations far outside your circle at first, as you won't be successful. Let your circle expand gradually, working with things that disturb you a little. You will soon have a large circle of comfort and peace. You will be relaxed with more of whatever life presents to you.

THE OFFICE

When I began working in the *ashram* office, my experience was gentler than when I started in the kitchen. I still had my issues to work with, but since the office was not so physically demanding as the kitchen, I didn't have the added exhaustion. This helped me to work with my edge where practice was more manageable. I was able to relax more with my fears and insecurities while I worked.

Although initially I had phone and registration tasks, as I handled the requests on the other end of the phone, my duties grew. Some days were extremely busy, taking care of many things at once. Sometimes they were slow and I didn't have much to do. That was an edge as well, since I was used to constant activity in the kitchen, and in my textile career. I would feel panic that I would be caught "not being busy." I also felt more lost during the slow times because I didn't have busyness to distract me.

During the first several months, I noticed a strong desire to learn everything immediately. I thought the sooner I learned all the new procedures, the sooner I would be comfortable. I realized I had been this way with all of my new jobs and tasks throughout my life. I would push myself hard to learn as quickly as possible so I could be comfortable.

This time I was aware of my behavior and allowed myself to be uncomfortable. When I panicked and started to rush or push myself, I stopped. I would be still for a moment, and breathe with the discomfort. I allowed myself to feel it. I would watch my thoughts and observe the sensations in my body. Using the breath helped me to calm down and stay with the process. Usually, within a few moments I would feel better. I repeated this process every time I found myself rushing and pushing.

Through all of it, busy or not, lost as to what was next, or trying to learn everything as fast as possible, I relaxed. I used my practice to just be present with what I was internally experiencing. As I did this, I noticed my circle of peace expanding. I felt a deeper level of comfort about more things. A situation would arise, and I would expect to feel the usual discomfort. I would be surprised as I noticed I felt fine. I could watch myself slowly become a new person who felt more at peace.

Another area of discomfort for me was the "to-do" list. Making lists has always helped me stay organized. I noticed that I felt restless or anxious when items couldn't be crossed off the list. When I did cross something off, I felt a sense of accomplishment and relief. The longer items stayed on the list, the more my discomfort increased. Another opportunity to relax!

One evening I was working late because I had been in meetings all day and got nothing else done. My "to-do" list was a mile long. I wasn't going to come close to finishing it even if I worked late. As I sat at my desk, plugging away on the list, I noticed that I felt calm.

In the recent past, I would have felt tense and anxious trying to get everything finished. That evening I simply prioritized, and worked on what was most important for my allotted time. I felt peaceful even though I was buried with tasks.

It is important to notice and take a minute to celebrate your progress. I may just give myself a mental pat on the back when I realize I have expanded my circle of peace. Sometimes I'll buy myself flowers, make my favorite meal, or some other appreciative gesture. Those moments of gratitude and appreciation for my work and growth help me to stick with it during the challenges.

SHIFTING AGAIN

After about six months in my office position, I started feeling comfortable, even a bit stagnant. I thought, "Oh no..." Sure enough, I got a new position. This time I became program director, with more responsibility. I went through a week of intense fear and incapability issues. This time I celebrated that it only lasted a week! In the past I would have felt uneasy for at least several months.

I applied the practice of consciously relaxing with the intense insecurity. I allowed myself to feel it, and even had an attitude of curiosity as I observed it. Since it was quite familiar, I thought, "Oh hello again, Fear, I know you well." This attitude of curiosity helped me remain detached as I felt it and relaxed with it. I noticed I could be uncomfortable and okay at the same time. This knowledge helped me move through the feelings.

As part of my program-director duties, I would sometimes manage a particular program, interacting directly with the guests. I enjoyed this the most, even though it meant working long days and on my time off. This became an experiment in expanding my capacity to serve others even while feeling tired. Sometimes I would think I could catch a break and rest, and then someone would need something from me. I experimented with taking care of myself and stretching my capacity to be present for others, regardless of how I felt. As I practiced relaxing with all people and circumstances, these experiments of increasing my capacity became fun.

As I continued to be present for whatever life put before me, I was able to show up in a more relaxed way. I could feel insecure or worried about failure, and let it shift into the background. While the background "noise" still occurred, I could do my work, teach, and serve others with a relaxed, confidant demeanor. **The trick was not to resist my fear and insecurity, and at the same time, not feed it with my attention.** I could accept how I showed up, and how life showed up.

Through this practice, I could more easily accept the parts of me I didn't like. When I didn't resist those parts, I quit feeding them with my attention and energy. I could experience my fears, insecurities, and inadequacies in my new relaxed way, which caused them to diminish. I didn't try to make them go away, yet they were going away. When I tried to overcome them, they were more dominant.

I noticed as I accepted myself more, I also accepted others more. Even if someone exhibited inappropriate behavior, I could notice it with compassion and acceptance. When I spoke to them from that place, the results were more effective. Accepting what was, meant that as I relaxed and loved myself, I could relax and love others.

Me, working with Gurudev

ASSISTING GURUDEV

After only three months as program director, life directed me to another area. I attended a meeting to discuss an upcoming program involving Gurudev. Right before I was about to begin the meeting, the *ashram* CEO started talking about administrative issues in Gurudev's office. I thought I was in the wrong meeting and that I should excuse myself. Oddly, it felt right to stay.

The next thing I heard was my name. The CEO informed Gurudev, and the others in his office, that I would join their team. That was the first anyone, including me, heard of the change. I was surprised at how calm I felt with this sudden turn of events. I trusted the situation, and agreed to the new position.

Working directly with Gurudev brought up my insecurities, but I was able to consciously relax with them. One of my first assignments was to plan his European trip. Gurudev and I contacted the people he knew throughout Europe. Soon he had offers to teach all over the continent. This was the first time I ever arranged a trip like this. I had no idea how far apart the different countries were, or whether it was best to take a train or plane.

During the entire time spent organizing that trip I felt the butterflies in my stomach, and the slight constriction in my upper abdomen and chest. I allowed myself to feel, without labeling the sensations or paying attention to my thoughts of "I don't know if I can do this." I could allow the doubts to float around in my mind as I observed them, without feeding them with attention. I allowed the sensations to exist as they were, without trying to push them away. As I relaxed with myself and the assignment, a flow of events happened which required less effort on my part.

Several of the contacts Gurudev planned to visit arranged transportation and accommodations. One, in particular, arranged much of the trip. As I continued to relax, making the next phone call, or sending the next email, the trip came together on its own. I became a vehicle for organizing the events and information, and didn't really have to do anything except whatever task came next. My trust and faith in life increased as I experienced situations taking care of themselves.

That was my process with everything I did in Gurudev's office. I relaxed with myself as I was, and with people and events as they were. Being relaxed does not mean I was always comfortable. In addition to contentment, I also relaxed with doubt, insecurity, being overwhelmed, and anything else that arose within me.

Working directly with Gurudev was a constant practice in surrender. I never knew what would be next, as he responds to the energy of the moment. Plans can change on a dime. What you expect often happens differently. Such as the first time I went on a day trip with him.

Gurudev received an invitation to speak at an Indian conference featuring a *swami*. After his speech, Gurudev was going to attend a friend's wedding. Originally, I wasn't going, as it was on my days off and I like my structure and free time. Nevertheless, he wanted me to accompany him, so I finally agreed to attend the wedding only, not the conference. I needed one day off!

I met him at the conference location for his morning lecture, and then we were to head to the wedding site. As the time approached for his lecture, it was clear nothing was on schedule. He would not be speaking at the appointed time. With every inquiry, we were told Gurudev would speak "soon." When "soon" kept getting later and later, I finally told Gurudev that if we stayed any longer we would miss the wedding. Gurudev said that was fine, the wedding wasn't as important as the conference.

For a moment, I felt tension and resistance within me. We can't be a no-show to a friend's wedding. The "plan" was to go to the wedding. The wedding was why I was here! I quickly withdrew my attention from those thoughts and relaxed with the sensations of resistance in my body. Within a minute, I felt neutral, and accepted that I was attending a conference, not a wedding. I was attending a conference that did not run according to schedule.

Almost everything at the conference was hours off the scheduled time. Even the events were different than described in the program. I was getting quite an education in Indian culture. I surrendered to reality, and let go of my concept and past experiences of conferences. I had a wonderful time as I enjoyed *this* conference.

A WEEK OF SURRENDER

After several months of assisting Gurudev, I had the opportunity to attend an *Ayurveda* conference with him in North Carolina. I was excited and nervous about the trip, as I had heard from others about the difficulties of traveling with Gurudev. I remembered Gurudev says we create our reality, so I decided to trust that my experience would be of my own creation, and what I needed for my spiritual evolution.

My intention going into the trip was to surrender. I would surrender to each moment, and do my best to be of service to Gurudev and his teachings. This practice turned out to be very powerful, giving me new appreciation for surrendering.

The first day of travel was beautiful, though, at times, overwhelming. I hadn't traveled in quite a while and had never been anyone's personal assistant, much less a *guru's*. I hoped I wouldn't get us lost on the way to Boone, that I hadn't forgotten to pack something I would need, that I brought the appropriate clothes, and worried over many other unimportant concerns.

After ten hours of travel we made it to the conference center and got settled. We looked around, registered, and attended one of the events. I had never heard of many of the people I met, whose names I couldn't pronounce, much less spell. I copied their names from their nametags and asked for business cards.

Gurudev had coached me on getting cards, handing out his bio and CV, catalogs, and articles. He told me what to take pictures of, which was almost everything, and reminded me to take notes. He reminded me to be alert and conscious. I had much to learn but he seemed to know I was doing my best.

At about 9:00 pm, we had tea with Dr. Frawley, an author of many books on yoga and *Ayurveda*, a good friend of Gurudev's. I had read some of his books, so was thrilled to be in his company. He has known Gurudev since the 70s, and talked about how Gurudev knows the true yoga that comes from divine energy, the life force.

I was grateful the conversation was fascinating, because the company I kept and the newness of my responsibilities overwhelmed me. At times, I could barely follow the conversation with the unfamiliar Vedic terminology, and was tired from the long day.

Eventually, we made it back to our hotel. It was late, and I worried for a moment I wouldn't have the energy for this work over the next several days. This day had started at 6:30 am and ended at 11:00 pm. I noticed how Gurudev just relaxed with each moment, one at a time. I trusted that if I were not the right person for this job I wouldn't be here.

I quickly withdrew my attention from my worry and focused on this moment rather than the whole trip at once. I remembered a saying of Gurudev's: "Don't eat the pantry, just what is on your plate." I focused on my breath and relaxed. Then I went to bed.

The next morning was the official start of the conference. I made breakfast for Gurudev and myself. Then I packed my bag with articles, catalogs, a camera, plus a variety of other things to promote Gurudev's teachings and message.

Throughout the day we listened to many presentations. During breaks, people introduced themselves to Gurudev and gave us their contact information. They invited him to present at other conferences and events, there were requests for interviews, and invitations to attend meetings. He always said, "Yes." I was learning to say the same.

It takes a while to get from one place to another when travelling with Gurudev because many people stop him to receive his blessings, his words of wisdom, his opinions or advise on their ideas, and many want pictures with him. He is patient and loving with each one. I surrendered to the slow process of getting from point A to point B. Many times, we didn't even make it to point B, instead, ending up at point C. I learned to be unattached to any plan or agenda.

As I became tired during the day, I would notice my mind thinking about how to control and manipulate a situation so I could take a break. I would think ahead, wondering if I could leave a presentation early to catch a nap. As soon as I noticed I was trying to control and get my way, I withdrew from the thoughts. I focused my attention on the pure sensations of feeling tired, on connecting to the person before me, on taking a picture, on doing whatever Gurudev needed. I let my will shift to the background and focused all my attention on the moment.

As I continually withdrew my attention from my thoughts of being tired, I felt the energy streaming through my body. I connected to my breath. This restored me, allowing me to remain alert. It allowed me to say "Yes" to serving Gurudev and the moment.

There were times I was able to take breaks. Those came from being in the moment and surrendering. I would notice an opportunity before me and see what would come of it. This was much different than trying to manipulate an opportunity, or plan to take a break. Events would be such that the chance for a break offered itself in the present moment, and I accepted.

One such opportunity presented itself over dinner the second night. It was getting quite late, yet everyone was still engaged in conversations. I noticed one of the people staying with us and remembered he drove separately. I asked him if he would give Gurudev a ride when he was ready to go. I excused myself and headed for bed. This way I took care of myself, and made sure Gurudev was taken care of, too.

Back at the hotel, I enjoyed a bath and thought about how nice it would be to sleep in a little the next day. Soon I heard a knock at the door. Gurudev informed me he had received an invitation to a private meeting with Sri Sri Ravi Shankar, a famous *swami* with over two and a half million followers, for the following morning at 7:30 am. This was a very special opportunity for Gurudev. I immediately withdrew from my thought of sleeping in and replied, "This is wonderful, Gurudev!" (Because it was.)

Gurudev arose very early the following morning. He was pacing around, turning lights on and off. I was reminded of an excited child who hopes that if he makes enough commotion, mom will wake up. I decided I might as well rise and start my practice. At 6:00 am, I heard a knock on my door.

"Ashvini, are you up?"

"Yes, Gurudev." (This is a phrase I use often.) "You can come in Gurudev."

He reminded me we needed to be ready by 7:30. I told him that was fine. He asked if I planned to eat breakfast. I replied that I would make oatmeal and join him in the dining room at 7:00 am.

Throughout that week, my days were a constant practice of saying, "Yes," to the moment, whether I was tired, overwhelmed, rested, or joyful. I surprised myself with my ability to withdraw from selfish thoughts, from fatigue, and from resistance. I allowed all of that to be there, without paying much attention to it. I was surprised at how saying, "Yes," and surrendering, fed me with joy. I noticed how I conserved my energy when I didn't control or manipulate to get my way. I ended up having one of the most amazing weeks of my life by surrendering and saying, "Yes."

Each time you surrender you are saying, "My Lord, thy will be done." You accept the gift of life, and allow it to lead you to the loving source that you are. However, in many cultures, especially mine, surrender is thought of as weak. "Turn the other cheek" is not too popular. I was therefore surprised to discover the power and strength in surrendering.

PRACTICE

It takes a practice to live in a relaxed way. The ego-mind is so used to running everything, and this creates tension. I have needed the tools of intention, Witnessing, feeling sensations, and breathing, to help me let go and move into trust. Without them, my mind would have kept me trapped in what I know, never allowing me the freedom of the unknown, of pure creativity. As I've practiced, and started experiencing the freedom and joy of spirit, it becomes easier to continue.

Your mind has imprisoned you. Your mind can also set you free. You just forget you have the key to your own freedom. Practice is the key. Use it. Let life guide you as you enjoy life. When you are not enjoying your life, use the practice to align yourself with reality and shift back into peace and joy.

When grief comes, use the practice to align with it without resisting. It will move out more quickly, and return you to peace sooner. When happiness and good times come, relax and enjoy the moment, instead of wondering how long it will last or what you can do to stay happy longer.

Whatever arises in each moment, allow yourself to experience it. Feeling pure sensations from the Witness, along with conscious breathing, allows you to experience life. **Practice is training to be present in this moment. Present with whatever this moment brings.**

This moment is the only place where God exists. How could God possibly be anywhere else? If God is in the past, then God is not here, because the past is gone. If God is in the future, then God is not here, because the future never arrives. **God is always here, in the present moment. To experience and connect with God, you also have to be in the present moment.**

I hope this book has been entertaining, as well as enlightening. My biggest hope is that you create your own practice. Otherwise, you will only be entertained by these words, and nothing will change for you. Practice and experience, along with understanding, is how change happens. As you align with your soul instead of your self-image, you become more relaxed, creative, and loving, because that is the true expression of your soul. **The self-image is selfish by nature, so it is only through the soul that you experience and express true love.**

When you walk away from something, moving toward your destination, all that is behind you shrinks until it disappears. What you are moving toward becomes larger until there is nothing else. Are you walking toward your ego, or are you walking toward God? Are you walking toward hate, or are you walking toward Love?

Do not resist what you are walking away from, just focus on where you are going. When you take a step backwards, notice, and then take a step forward. Before long, you will spend more time walking forward, toward your divine source. If you stop, that's okay. You know how to resume.

About the Author

Kenyon Gatlin is a teacher, speaker, and author in the field of stress reduction and yoga. She recently authored her first book, *Relax With Life*, about applying yoga principles to reduce stress. This is a practical "how to" book on incorporating spiritual teachings into your daily life.

Gatlin received her Bachelor of Fine Arts and Teachers Certificate for K – 12, from The University of North Carolina Greensboro, in 1993. After teaching art in public schools for a few years, she entered a successful fourteen-year career designing fabric for the home furniture industry, achieving senior designer status with one of the finest manufacturing companies in the world.

Although Gatlin thrived professionally in her art career, she spent much of her life searching for deeper meaning and spiritual connection, which led her to the practice of yoga in the late nineties. In 2002, Gatlin began teaching yoga in addition to her textile career. When she met her *Guru*, teacher *Yogi* Amrit Desai, in 2005, her practice catapulted her into spiritual transformation.

After going through a divorce and ending her design career, Gatlin moved to *Yogi* Desai's *ashram* in 2012, where she continues to study and teach yoga. Through her studies, and various positions at the *ashram*, Gatlin embodies the spiritual teachings of yoga, using them to reduce stress and relax with everything life presents.

Gatlin has taught people of all races, religions, ages, and states of health at yoga studios, hospitals, and corporations. Her teaching style is simple, engaging, and experiential, inspiring you to see, know, and experience your true spiritual nature. Her passion is helping others apply spiritual truths, in a practical way, to their daily life to achieve inner fulfillment and peace.

Gatlin is certified as a 200 and 500 registered yoga teacher. She holds certifications in the Amrit Method of Yoga Therapy, as well as in Yoga Therapy for cancer and chronic illness through Integral Yoga. Gatlin is a facilitator of the Amrit Method of Yoga *Nidra* and an Amrit Method Reiki Master. She currently teaches at The Amrit Yoga Institute.

Acknowledgements

Much of this book is based in the teachings of my *Guru Yogi* Amrit Desai and his daughter Kamini Desai. I am forever grateful for their dedication to the authentic teachings of yoga which have freed me from so much tension, worry and stress.

When I embarked on this book journey many kindly offered me their friendship and support. I thank John Hlavinka who encouraged me to begin. Laura Gushin, Chris Tibbits, Wanda Cox, Kathy Kennedy, Sue Dennison, Ralph LaPerch, Susan Freeman all read early drafts and offered helpful suggestions. Russ Mobley helped design the book cover, took the pictures in my book and offered encouragement and support through out the publishing process.

Of course this book could not have happened without the experiences I wrote about. I am grateful for everyone in this book and the role they played in my spiritual growth. I will not name them to preserve their privacy but I am nevertheless grateful for their huge contribution to the book and my life.

I am grateful to my parents JoAnn and Roger Gatlin who have supported me in many ways throughout my life including their financial support in bringing this book to the public.

Glossary of Terms

Ashram- A spiritual community following the teachings of a Master or *Guru*

Breath- The main carrier of energy.

Chair Pose- In Amrit Yoga "Chair Pose" is called "Standing Squat Pose"

Conscious- a waking state where you are aware of your thoughts, feelings and actions.

Edge- the point where your ability to relax intersects with your tendency to react

Goal- a result you want to achieve

Guru- someone who has traveled the spiritual path you are on, and can connect you to inner wisdom

Integration- to bring parts together to create a whole. Thinking, feeling, and doing come together so you are total and present.

Intention- the direction you want to travel toward

Light- illuminates

Meditation- a state of being entered through a continued period of concentration on a single object.

Polarity- complimentary opposites, (hot is not against cold, they co-exist)

Prana- energy, life force, Holy Spirit

Reaction- fight or flight response. Can be subtle like rolling the eyes or complaining.

Relax- absence of tension and stress

Savasana- a resting pose in yoga, usually done at the end of a class lying down. Savasana literally means Corpse Pose because you are still as a corpse.

Subconscious- where our unconscious past memories and experiences that influence our behavior are stored. The subconscious is in harmony with nature but gets superimposed with our unconscious beliefs.

Tapas- is a Sanskrit word meaning "to burn". It is sometimes defined as discipline because it takes discipline to feel the burn.

Third eye- Is located at the center of the forehead between the eyebrows. This area lines up with the Pineal Gland at the center of the brain. The Pineal Gland is also referred to as the third eye.

Unconscious- a waking state where you are unaware of your thoughts, feelings and actions. You live from automatic pilot and habit patterns.

Witness- An objective silent observer. Watches but doesn't participate.

Yoga- is a Sanskrit word for union. Being fully present and absorbed in the moment.

Yoga Nidra- literally means *yogic* sleep. It is a guided relaxation meditation that allows you to access the deep restorative states of sleep while remaining conscious. Thirty minutes of yoga *nidra* is equivalent to three hours of restful sleep.

Resources

RECOMMENDED READING

After the Ecstasy the Laundry- Jack Kornfield

Bhagavad Gita- Hindu scripture

English Standard Version Holy Bible

The Places that Scare You- Pema Chodron

The Power of Now- Eckhart Tolle

The Yoga Sutras of Patanjali

Yoga and Ayurveda: Self-Healing and Self- Realization- Dr. David Frawley

WEBSITES

HeartMath Institute- global leader in emotional physiology and stress- management
http://www.heartmath.org/research/research-home/research-center-home.html

❋

Article on the electrical magnetic field of the heart:
http://www.heartmath.org/free-services/articles-of-the-
heart/energetic-heart-is-unfolding.html

The Amrit Yoga Institute
www.amrityoga.org

www.kenyongatlin.com